READINGS ON

JULIUS CAESAR

Other titles in the Greenhaven Press Literary Companion Series:

American Authors

Maya Angelou
Stephen Crane
Emily Dickinson
William Faulkner
F. Scott Fitzgerald
Nathaniel Hawthorne
Ernest Hemingway
Herman Melville
Arthur Miller
Eugene O'Neill
Edgar Allan Poe
John Steinbeck
Mark Twain
Thornton Wilder

American Literature

The Adventures of Huckleberry Finn
The Adventures of Tom Sawyer
The Catcher in the Rye
The Crucible
Death of a Salesman
The Glass Menagerie
The Grapes of Wrath
The Great Gatsby
Of Mice and Men
The Old Man and the Sea
The Pearl
The Scarlet Letter
A Separate Peace

British Authors

Jane Austen
Joseph Conrad
Charles Dickens

British Literature

Animal Farm
Beowulf
The Canterbury Tales
Great Expectations
Hamlet
Lord of the Flies
Macbeth
Pride and Prejudice
Romeo and Juliet
Shakespeare: The Comedies
Shakespeare: The Histories
Shakespeare: The Sonnets
Shakespeare: The Tragedies
A Tale of Two Cities
Wuthering Heights

World Authors

Fyodor Dostoyevsky
Homer
Sophocles

World Literature

All Quiet on the Western Front
The Diary of a Young Girl
A Doll's House

THE GREENHAVEN PRESS
Literary Companion
TO BRITISH LITERATURE

READINGS ON

JULIUS CAESAR

Don Nardo, *Book Editor*

David L. Bender, *Publisher*
Bruno Leone, *Executive Editor*
Bonnie Szumski, *Series Editor*

Greenhaven Press, Inc., San Diego, CA

Every effort has been made to trace the owners of copy-
righted material. The articles in this volume may have
been edited for content, length, and/or reading level. The
titles have been changed to enhance the editorial purpose.
Those interested in locating the original source will find
the complete citation on the first page of each article.

Library of Congress Cataloging-in-Publication Data

Readings on Julius Caesar / Don Nardo, book editor.
     p.   cm. — (The Greenhaven Press literary
companion to British literature)
    Includes bibliographical references and index.
    ISBN 1-56510-853-1 (lib. bdg. : alk. paper). —
ISBN 1-56510-852-3 (pbk. : alk. paper)
    1. Shakespeare, William, 1564–1616. Julius Caesar.
2. Caesar, Julius–In literature. 3. Rome–In literature.
4. Tragedy. I. Nardo, Don, 1947–   . II. Series.
PR2808.R42   1999
822.3'3—dc21   98-29762
                                          CIP

Cover photo: © Hulton Getty/Tony Stone Images

Copyright ©1999 by Greenhaven Press, Inc.
PO Box 289009
San Diego, CA 92198-9009
Printed in the U.S.A.

"Why, man, he doth bestride
the narrow world
Like a Colossus, and we petty
men
Walk under his huge legs, and
peep about
To find ourselves dishonorable
graves.
Men at some time are
masters of their fates;
The fault, dear Brutus, is not in
our stars,
But in ourselves, that we are
underlings."

Cassius to Brutus in Act I, Scene 2 of
William Shakespeare's Julius Caesar

CONTENTS

Chapter 2: Brutus, the Pivotal Character

Chapter 3: Other Important Characters in *Julius Caesar*

over Brutus and makes the conspiracy a reality. By contrast, Antony sits back and waits for the right opportunity to strike back at the assassins and in the process to gain power for himself.

The great Roman senator and orator, Marcus Tullius Cicero, was in Rome at the time of Caesar's assassination, but he did not take part in the deed. Shakespeare pays homage to Cicero by making him a minor character in the play. However, Shakespeare's Cicero and the real Cicero, though similar in many respects, were not quite the same person.

Chapter 4: The Unifying Themes of Political Power and Oratory

In *Julius Caesar,* Shakespeare brilliantly explores the weapons, tactics, and potential dangers of the game of political power in ancient Rome. He shows how grasping, ambitious men used the power of words, as well as the force of their personalities, to achieve and hold onto power. In so doing, he refrains from overtly endorsing either Caesar's or the conspirators' agenda, revealing that each had both strengths and flaws.

Antony's "Friends, Romans, countrymen" speech to the mob in the Roman Forum is perhaps the most famous example of the power of persuasive speech in all of literature. *Julius Caesar* abounds in other examples of speech-making, both public and private, used to convince, manipulate, and gain advantage and power.

When Brutus addresses the crowd in the Forum after the assassination, he claims that he slew Caesar because the dictator was ambitious, fully expecting his hearers to sympathize with the deed. But thanks to the much more effective speech Antony delivers a few minutes later, the mob turns with a vengeance on Brutus and the other conspirators. Here, Shakespeare masterfully demonstrates how a skillful speaker can bend others to his own will and change the course of history.

Chapter 5: Other Dramatic Themes and Images in *Julius Caesar*

FOREWORD

The story's bare facts are simple: The captain, an old and scarred seafarer, walks with a peg leg made of whale ivory. He relentlessly drives his crew to hunt the world's oceans for the great white whale that crippled him. After a long search, the ship encounters the whale and a fierce battle ensues. Finally the captain drives his harpoon into the whale, but the harpoon line catches the captain about the neck and drags him to his death.

A simple story, a straightforward plot—yet, since the 1851 publication of Herman Melville's *Moby-Dick*, readers and critics have found many meanings in the struggle between Captain Ahab and the whale. To some, the novel is a cautionary tale that depicts how Ahab's obsession with revenge leads to his insanity and death. Others believe that the whale represents the unknowable secrets of the universe and that Ahab is a tragic hero who dares to challenge fate by attempting to discover this knowledge. Perhaps Melville intended Ahab as a criticism of Americans' tendency to become involved in well-intentioned but irrational causes. Or did Melville model Ahab after himself, letting his fictional character express his anger at what he perceived as a cruel and distant god?

Although literary critics disagree over the meaning of *Moby-Dick*, readers do not need to choose one particular interpretation in order to gain an understanding of Melville's novel. Instead, by examining various analyses, they can gain numerous insights into the issues that lie under the surface of the basic plot. Studying the writings of literary critics can also aid readers in making their own assessments of *Moby-Dick* and other literary works and in developing analytical thinking skills.

The Greenhaven Literary Companion Series was created with these goals in mind. Designed for young adults, this unique anthology series provides an engaging and comprehensive introduction to literary analysis and criticism. The essays included in the Literary Companion Series are chosen for their accessibility to a young adult audience and are expertly edited in consideration of both the reading and comprehension levels of this audience. In addition, each essay is introduced by a concise summation that presents the contributing writer's main themes and insights. Every anthology in the Literary Companion Series contains a varied selection of critical essays that cover a wide time span and express diverse views. Wherever possible, primary sources are represented through excerpts from authors' notebooks, letters, and journals and through contemporary criticism.

Each title in the Literary Companion Series pays careful consideration to the historical context of the particular author or literary work. In-depth biographies and detailed chronologies reveal important aspects of authors' lives and emphasize the historical events and social milieu that influenced their writings. To facilitate further research, every anthology includes primary and secondary source bibliographies of articles and/or books selected for their suitability for young adults. These engaging features make the Greenhaven Literary Companion series ideal for introducing students to literary analysis in the classroom or as a library resource for young adults researching the world's great authors and literature.

Exceptional in its focus on young adults, the Greenhaven Literary Companion Series strives to present literary criticism in a compelling and accessible format. Every title in the series is intended to spark readers' interest in leading American and world authors, to help them broaden their understanding of literature, and to encourage them to formulate their own analyses of the literary works that they read. It is the editors' hope that young adult readers will find these anthologies to be true companions in their study of literature.

INTRODUCTION

An authoritarian and seemingly very confident man dressed in a toga enters ancient Rome's venerable Senate chamber. Several senators, also wearing togas, crowd around this stately father-figure, some of them pleading for favors. Then, without warning, one of them draws a dagger from beneath his robes and plunges it into the father-figure. A number of others follow suit, stabbing him repeatedly as he valiantly struggles to stay on his feet. There is a momentary lull as he recognizes one of the assassins, directly confronts the man, and with a mixture of surprise and deep regret asks, "You too?" Then the mortally wounded father-figure falls dead and his murderers proceed to wash their hands in his blood.

This scene, endlessly repeated on stage, in films and novels, and in satires and cartoons, is familiar to virtually everyone in Western society, regardless of educational level. Even those who know nothing else about Rome or ancient history can identify the murdered father-figure as Julius Caesar, the great Roman general and arguably one of the four or five most famous people who ever lived. Many know also that the man he confronts seconds before collapsing is his friend, Brutus, who has turned against him. The themes of an all-powerful ruler being struck down by those seeking liberty and of personal betrayal are so universal that they make the scene immediate and understandable to anyone in any time period or culture. More importantly, the scene has added power because, as everyone knows, it actually happened. Caesar was indeed stabbed to death by Brutus and other conspirators in the Roman Senate on March 15, 44 B.C.

Yet when stage and film directors, writers, and satirists reenact Caesar's untimely end, it is usually not the historical event itself that inspires their depictions; rather, they almost always draw on one particular version of that famous event, namely the play, *Julius Caesar*, written in 1599 by William Shakespeare. Shakespeare's dramatization of the true story of Caesar's fall has been so often performed, imitated, and read by school children and scholars alike, that it has become part of the Western public consciousness. In this regard, one of the play's lines has proved ironic. In Act 3, Scene 1, just after Caesar's assassination, Brutus's fellow conspirator, Cassius, says, "How many ages hence shall this our lofty scene be acted over in states unborn and accents unknown!" Shakespeare here intended to emphasize that the conspirators viewed their deed as momentous enough to be remembered and dramatized in succeeding ages. It is doubtful that he realized that over time the line would take on added meaning as a reference to the many thousands of performances of his own play about Caesar.

Many of these performances have been, as they were when Shakespeare was still living, staged by professionals. Some of the greatest actors of each generation have played one or all of the play's four major roles—Caesar, Brutus, Cassius, and Antony—on stage, in settings ranging from lavish reproductions of ancient Rome, to modern fascist states, to bare platforms. The play has also spawned many films, the most famous being the 1953 version starring James Mason as Brutus and Marlon Brando as Antony. The number of large-scale professional productions pales, however, before that of amateur stagings, especially in boys' schools, which are partially attracted to the play because of its long list of meaty male roles. Another factor that makes *Julius Caesar* appealing to performers, both professional and amateur, is the language. The play contains some of Shakespeare's most famous, colorful, and dramatic lines and speeches, including Cassius's "The fault, dear Brutus, is not in our stars, but in ourselves," Caesar's "Coward's die many times before their deaths," and Antony's immortal "Friends, Romans, countrymen, lend me your ears!" The play is also universally recognized as one of the two or three greatest political dramas ever written. For these reasons, it is likely to retain its important place in the Western dramatic repertoire for as long as the names of Caesar and Shakespeare remain household words.

The essays selected for the Greenhaven Literary Companion to Shakespeare's *Julius Caesar* provide teachers and students with a wide range of information and opinion about the play and its author's style, themes, and outlook on the human condition. All of the authors of the essays are or were (until their deaths) noted professors at leading colleges and universities and/or scholars specializing in Shakespearean studies. Among this companion volume's several special features: each of the essays explains or discusses in detail a specific, narrowly focused topic; the introduction to each essay previews the main points; and inserts interspersed within the essays serve as examples of ideas expressed by the authors, offer supplementary information, and/or add authenticity and color. These inserts come from *Julius Caesar* or other plays by Shakespeare, from critical commentary about these works, or from other scholarly sources. Overall, this book is designed to supplement the reading of the play itself, to enhance the reader's understanding and enjoyment of one of the most powerful and enduring literary works ever created.

WILLIAM SHAKESPEARE: A BIOGRAPHY

Not long before attempting to dramatize Caesar's fall from power and glory, Shakespeare wrote and produced several plays about what was then recent English history. These included *Richard II, Richard III, Henry IV, Parts 1* and *2,* and *Henry V.* Little exposition (passages explaining background and characters) was needed in these works because his audience was already intimately acquainted with the main events and figures of the nation's history. In fact, it is likely that even the least educated theatergoers of the day had a far stronger grasp of history and their place within it than today's average American does.

THE BACKGROUND—CAESAR'S RISE TO POWER

Shakespeare's audience was just as interested in and conversant about the great events and characters of Roman history as it was about its English counterparts. So in approaching Caesar's story, the playwright once again found no need to encumber the play with lengthy explanatory speeches. The beginning of *Julius Caesar* is set in Rome early in 44 B.C., shortly before Caesar's assassination; the work ends not long afterwards on the plain of Philippi, in northern Greece, immediately following the bloody defeat of Caesar's murderers. As for the background exposition and basic information needed to understand and enjoy the play, most of Shakespeare's spectators knew that the real Caesar was born about 100 B.C. into a well-to-do Roman family. It was also common knowledge that Caesar was a patrician, a member of the prestigious land-owning elite that had founded the Roman Republic over four hundred years before (in 509 B.C. to be exact).

Most members of Shakespeare's audience were equally aware that as a young man Caesar slowly and methodically worked his way up the ladder of Roman political offices, serving as a treasurer-paymaster, an organizer of public games, and a judge. Caesar's ultimate goal was to match, and hopefully to surpass, the power and influence of the two most formidable Roman strongmen of the day: popular military general Gnaeus Pompey and millionaire financier Marcus Crassus. Shakespeare makes reference to Pompey's popularity in the first scene of *Julius Caesar*, when the military officer Marullus reminds a congregation of Romans about how they used to climb up to the "chimney-tops" to "see great Pompey pass the streets of Rome."[1] Demonstrating the remarkable tactical skills that would characterize his later political and military maneuvers, Caesar decided to work with, rather than against, his rivals, Pompey and Crassus. In the summer of 60 B.C., he engineered a secret alliance with them, the uneasy but powerful partnership that later became known as the First Triumvirate.[2]

The Triumvirate's power showed itself almost immediately. With the support of Pompey and Crassus, Caesar was elected as one of the two consuls, or administrator-generals, who ran the state, ostensibly under the Senate's guidance. But Caesar paid little or no attention to the Senate. His entire term as consul was marked by bullying, intimidation, and illegal tactics. Staunch republicans had long worried that the rise of powerful individuals might threaten or even destroy the state, and the advent of the Triumvirate transformed that worry into alarm.

After his term as consul had ended, Caesar used his influence to get himself appointed governor of the Roman province in the southern part of Gaul, what is now France. He realized that he still lacked the military experience and backing to challenge Pompey and reasoned that he could acquire both while conquering the wild non-Roman lands of central and northern Gaul. During eight years of hard and often brilliant campaigning, Caesar achieved his goal. He fought alongside his men, proving the uncommon courage alluded to by Shakespeare in the speech Caesar recites just before his fateful trip to the Senate:

> Cowards die many times before their deaths,
> The valiant never taste of death but once.
> Of all the wonders that I yet have heard,
> It seems to me most strange that men should fear,
> Seeing that death, a necessary end,
> Will come when it will come.[3]

Displaying this bold attitude, along with a healthy measure of tactical genius, Caesar managed to build a loyal personal army while bringing Gaul into Rome's empire and thereby bolstering his popularity and political power.

The extent of that power worried the Senate more than ever. In January 49 B.C., it ordered Caesar to disband his army at once, but he refused. Boldly defying the Senate, he led his troops to the Rubicon River, the formal boundary between the northern provinces and Italy proper. According to the later Roman historian Suetonius, Caesar told his officers, "We may still draw back but, once across that little bridge, we shall have to fight it out. . . . Let us accept [the signs] from the gods, and follow where they beckon, in vengeance on our doubling-dealing enemies. The die is cast."[4] With these words, Caesar crossed the Rubicon and plunged the Roman world into a disastrous civil war.

Caesar Murdered and Avenged

As the playgoers who watched *Julius Caesar* in Shakespeare's day knew well, Caesar ultimately won the war, a victory that soon led him into the circumstances depicted in the play's opening scenes. Having totally defeated his former colleague, Pompey (Crassus had died before the war), and most of his other rivals, he celebrated four magnificent victory parades in the capital in October 46 B.C. Militarily and politically, his position was firm and unchallenged and he might have used his tremendous powers to lead the Roman commonwealth into a new and constructive era. However, many old-guard republicans became outraged when Caesar made himself dictator for life, began transacting business on a throne of ivory and gold, and accepted religious dedications that referred to him as a god. "This man is now become a god," the bitter senator Gaius Cassius complains to his colleague, Marcus Brutus, in the opening of Shakespeare's play, "and Cassius is a wretched creature, and must bend his body [bow] if Caesar carelessly but nod on him."[5] Fearing that Caesar would go a step further and declare himself king, a title most Romans heartily despised, a group of senators, led by Cassius and Brutus, took desperate action. Their now famous attack, which Shakespeare made the dramatic centerpiece of his play, occurred in the Senate chamber on the 15th, or "Ides," of March, 44 B.C. According to Suetonius,

> as soon as Caesar took his seat the conspirators crowded around him as if to pay their respects. Tillius Cimber . . . came up close, pretending to ask a question. Caesar made a gesture of postponement, but Cimber caught hold of his shoulders. "This is violence!" Caesar cried, and . . . as he turned away, one of the Casca brothers with a sweep of his dagger stabbed

him just below the throat. . . . Twenty-three dagger thrusts
went home as he stood there. Caesar did not utter a sound after Casca's blow had drawn a groan from him; though some
say that when he saw Marcus Brutus about to deliver the second blow, he reproached him in Greek with: "You, too, my
child?" The entire Senate then dispersed in confusion, and
Caesar was left lying dead for some time until three slave boys
carried him home in a litter [stretcher], with one arm hanging
over the side.[6]

After the assassination, the conspirators ran into the
streets proclaiming liberty. They thought that killing Caesar
would restore the integrity and power of their beloved Republic. But they naively failed to recognize that it was the
government's very lack of authority and flexibility that had
allowed Caesar to intimidate it. His demise created a sudden
but temporary vacuum at the pinnacle of Roman politics, a
vacuum that would be immediately filled by other powerful
men. The first of these men to step forward was Caesar's former assistant, Mark Antony. As Shakespeare dutifully chronicles in the play, Antony was quickly followed by Caesar's
adopted son (and great-nephew), Octavian, and a popular
general named Marcus Lepidus.

First, Antony turned the Roman mob against the conspirators, as Shakespeare so memorably dramatized in the famous
"Friends, Romans, countrymen" speech. "Great Caesar fell,"
Antony tells the crowd. "O, what a fall was there, my countrymen! / Then I, and you, and all of us fell down, / Whilst bloody
treason flourished over us."[7] Thus, only hours after striking
Caesar down, the assassins found their dream of restoring sen-
atorial power collapsing around them. Hearing of the approach
of the angry crowds, most of them fled Italy and took refuge in
Greece, where Brutus and Cassius began raising troops with
which they hoped to restore the Senate's and their own prestige
and authority. They did not bargain for the formation of a new
triumvirate, composed of three powerful rivals—Antony, Octavian, and Lepidus—in the winter of 43 B.C.

The inevitable showdown between the old guard and the
new took the form of two pitched battles, separated by an in-
terval of three weeks, at Philippi in October 42 B.C.[8] According to the second-century A.D. Greek historian Appian, as the
ranks of the opposing forces faced each other in the decisive
second encounter, all involved knew that the fate of the Republic was at stake.

[The soldiers] did not now remember that they were fellow-
citizens of their enemies, but hurled threats at each other as

though they had been enemies by birth and descent, so much did the anger of the moment extinguish reason and nature in them. Both sides divined [realized] equally that this day and this battle would decide the fate of Rome completely; and so indeed it did.[9]

The struggle at Philippi, which Appian later described as "superb and terrible," was a drawn-out and bloody affair. In the end, Antony's and Octavian's forces won, leaving the former conspirators hopeless and humiliated.[10] Rather than surrender, Brutus and Cassius committed suicide, and the last credible chance of restoring the Republic died with them. As Shakespeare showed in his play's powerful finale, even in death Caesar had triumphed. "Caesar, thou art revenged," cries Cassius in his own death agonies, "even with the sword that killed thee."[11] This and the play's other lines were composed some 1,640 years after the actual events took place; yet it is probable that Shakespeare's magnificent dramatization captures the essence, if not the exact words, the real Cassius, Brutus, and Caesar spoke.

AN ERA OF CHANGE AND RESTLESSNESS

The stories, fates, and legends of Caesar and Shakespeare converged during a particularly crucial historical time and place—namely England in the last decades of the sixteenth century. Because Queen Elizabeth I sat on England's throne, the era roughly coinciding with her reign (1558–1603) is referred to as the Elizabethan Age. This period proved to be one of the richest, most dynamic, and most opportune cultural and professional settings for aspiring poets and dramatists in all of Western history. A bevy of great and famous writers, among them Francis Bacon, Christopher Marlowe, Ben Jonson, and John Donne, were all born within a dozen years of Shakespeare's birth and published works during his lifetime. Playwriting was emerging as a legitimate art form, as evidenced partly by the construction of England's first public theater when Shakespeare was twelve. Not long afterward, Raphael Holinshed's *Chronicles of England, Scotlande, and Irelande,* and the first English translation of the *Parallel Lives,* the first-century A.D. Greek historian Plutarch's biographies of famous ancient Greeks and Romans, were published. These would later become the sources for the plots and characters of many of Shakespeare's greatest plays.

The times in which Shakespeare was born were also marked by rapid and momentous political, social, and economic transformation, as powerful European nations like England greatly expanded their horizons. It was "an era of change and restlessness," remarks Shakespearean scholar Karl Holzknecht.

> Everywhere—in religion, in philosophy, in politics, in science, in literature—new ideas were springing into life and coming into conflict with the established order of things. . . . A whole series of events and discoveries, coming together at the end of the fifteenth century [just preceding the Elizabethan age], transformed . . . many of the institutions and the habits of mind that we call medieval. The gradual break-up of feudalism . . . the discovery of gunpowder and. . . the mariner's compass and the possibility of safely navigating the limitless ocean, the production of paper and the invention of printing, and . . . the Copernican system of astronomy which formulated a new center of the universe—all of these new conceptions had a profound effect upon human thought and became the foundations for intellectual, moral, social, and economic changes which quickly made themselves felt.[12]

To these forces that shaped Europe in the 1500s can be added many important English historical events that occurred during Shakespeare's own lifetime. In 1587, when he was about twenty-three, Queen Elizabeth beheaded her distant relative and rival for the throne, Mary, queen of Scots. The following year an English fleet halted an attempted invasion of England by defeating the mighty Spanish Armada. Sir Francis Drake, Sir John Hawkins, and other adventurous English sea captains helped to turn the sea lanes into great highways for England's growing naval power. And in 1607 English settlers founded the colony of Jamestown in Virginia, giving England a foothold in the New World. England's command of the sea brought it commercial success and its ports and cities became bustling centers of high finance, social life, and the arts. Amid all of this, the theater, increasingly recognized as an art form, provided a fertile creative atmosphere for the efforts and innovations of young playwrights like Ben Jonson and Will Shakespeare.

AN INDIVIDUAL "LEARNED IN HUMAN NATURE"

Elizabeth's tumultuous reign was in its twelfth year when Shakespeare was born in 1564 in Stratford, now called Stratford-upon-Avon, a village in Warwickshire County in central England. The exact day is somewhat uncertain, but tradition accepts it as April 23. If correct, it is part of an unusual coincidence, for April 23 is also the supposed month and day of Shakespeare's death fifty-two years later.[13] These dates and other facts relating to Shakespeare's life have survived in over one hundred official documents, including entries about him and his relatives in parish registers and town archives, legal records involving property transfers, and business letters to or about him. More than fifty allusions to Shakespeare and his works appear in the published writings of his contemporaries. These sources do not tell us much about Shakespeare's personality, likes and dislikes, and personal beliefs. Yet they provide enough information to piece together a concise outline of the highlights of his life and career.

At the time Will Shakespeare was born, his father, John Shakespeare, was a glover and perhaps also a wool and leather dealer in Stratford. The elder Shakespeare also held various local community positions, among them ale taster, town councilman, town treasurer, and eventually bailiff, or mayor. John and his wife, Mary Arden, were married shortly before Queen Elizabeth ascended to the English throne in 1558; they subsequently produced eight children, of whom Will was the third child and eldest son.

Nothing definite is known about William Shakespeare's childhood. It is fairly certain, however, that between the ages of seven and sixteen he attended the town grammar school. There, students studied Latin grammar and literature, including the works of the Roman writers Terence, Cicero, Virgil, and Ovid, as well as works by later European authors such as the Dutch moralist Erasmus. In addition to these formal studies, Shakespeare must have done much reading on his own time when in his teens and twenties. We know this because his works reveal a knowledge not only of Latin but also of French and several other languages. Shakespeare was also well versed in both ancient and recent European history, as shown by his intimate familiarity with Plutarch's *Parallel Lives* and the works of Holinshed and other English chroniclers. Shakespeare read a great deal of fiction, too, including the classic works of Italy's Giovanni Boccaccio and England's Geoffrey Chaucer.

Besides what he learned in school and from his reading, Shakespeare also acquired a great deal of practical knowledge about life. His writings clearly show that he was familiar with the most intimate details of the royal court, the trades, the army, the church, as well as the mannerisms and aspirations of people of all ages and walks of life. The eighteenth-century English novelist Henry Fielding described him as "learned in human nature."[14] Even if most of what Shakespeare knew was self-taught, he was certainly a supremely educated individual.

The first certain fact about Shakespeare after his birth is the date on which his marriage license was issued—November 27, 1582, as recorded in volume thirty-two of the bishop of Worcester's *Register*. The bride, who was eight years older than Shakespeare, was Anne Hathaway, the daughter of a farmer from the nearby village of Shottery. Most modern scholars believe that the wedding itself took place in Temple Grafton, a village about five miles from Stratford (since Temple Grafton is mentioned in the entry in the *Register*). Other local documents reveal a daughter, Susanna, christened May 26, 1583, and twins, Hamnet and Judith, christened February 26, 1585; other surviving records show that Hamnet died in 1596 at the age of eleven.

The exact reason why young Will Shakespeare chose the theater as a profession is not known. But it stands to reason that he was moved by and greatly attracted to the traveling acting companies that visited Stratford, as well as other nearby towns, on a periodic basis. Stratford records show that the theatrical troupes the Queen's Men and the Earl of Worcester's Men performed in the town in 1568 and 1569, when Shakespeare was about five. Whatever the reason for being "bitten by the acting bug," in 1587, when he was about twenty-three, he struck out for London to try his luck in the theater.[15]

Various undocumented stories have survived about the young man's first professional job. One maintains that he tended horses outside a theater until offered the position of assistant prompter. Another suggests that a member of a prominent theatrical company, perhaps the Queen's Men, was severely injured in a brawl and Shakespeare volunteered (or was enlisted) to act in the unfortunate fellow's place. This scenario is not as far-fetched as it might seem. Experience was usually not a prerequisite for actors assigned to small roles, and the majority of young players learned the theatrical "ropes" on the job.

It appears that Shakespeare learned quicker than most. By 1593 he had written *Richard III*, *The Comedy of Errors*, and *Henry VI, Parts 1, 2,* and *3*, earning him a solid reputation as a playwright and an actor in the London theater scene. At first he did not attach himself exclusively to any specific theatrical company; instead he worked on and off with several, including that of Richard Burbage, the finest and most acclaimed actor of the time. Burbage, four years younger than Shakespeare, became the playwright's close friend and colleague and eventually played the title roles in the original productions of some of his greatest plays, including *Hamlet, Richard III, King Lear,* and *Othello.* During these early years in London, Shakespeare wrote two long poems, *Venus and Adonis* (1593) and *Lucrece* (1594), which established him as an accepted and respectable literary figure. By contrast, his plays, like those of other playwrights of the time, were viewed as popular but low-brow entertainment rather than as legitimate literature.

The founding of Lord Chamberlain's Company in 1594 marked an important turning point in Shakespeare's career. This theatrical troupe performed at all the major theaters of the day, including the Theatre, the Swan, and the Curtain (the famous Globe had not yet been built). Shakespeare joined the group and stayed with it throughout his career. When it became known as the King's Servants in 1603, it was performing periodically at the royal court and Shakespeare was a shareholder in all company profits.

As a permanent member of the company, Shakespeare had the opportunity to work regularly with the best English actors of the day. In addition to the great Burbage, these included Henry Condell, John Heminge, William Sly, and Will Kempe. Kempe, one of the great comic players of the Elizabethan stage, specialized in broad, slapstick comedy and physical clowning. Over the years Shakespeare wrote a number of comic roles especially for Kempe, among them Costard in *Love's Labors Lost,* Launce in *The Two Gentlemen of Verona,* and Bottom in *A Midsummer Night's Dream.* After Kempe left the company in 1600 another talented comedic actor, Robert Armin, took his place. For Armin, Shakespeare wrote the parts of Touchstone in *As You Like It* and the fool in *King Lear.*

From 1594 on, Shakespeare devoted most of his time to writing plays, although he supposedly occasionally took small roles in productions of his and his colleagues' works. According to tradition, for instance, he played the ghost in *Hamlet* and the old servant, Adam, in *As You Like It.* Between 1594 and 1601 Shakespeare composed a long list of plays of amazing variety and quality. Among them were the comedies *The Taming of the Shrew, The Two Gentlemen of Verona, The Merry Wives of Windsor,* and *Twelfth Night;* the histories *Richard II, Henry IV, Parts 1* and *2,* and *Henry V;* and the tragedies *Romeo and Juliet, Hamlet,* and *Julius Caesar.*

ONSTAGE SPLENDOR AND PAGEANTRY

While he was turning out these masterpieces, Shakespeare also came to be part owner in what turned out to be one of

the most famous theaters ever built. In 1597 he and his colleagues in Lord Chamberlain's Company encountered difficulty in renewing their lease at the Theatre playhouse and
decided to build their own theater. It took them only eight
months to construct the Globe Theatre on the south side of
the Thames River and to close a joint ownership deal with Sir
Nicholas Brend, who owned the property. This marked the
first known instance in theatrical history of actors owning
the theater in which they performed.

It was for this theater and the specific properties of its
stage that Shakespeare tailored the plays he wrote in the
years that followed. The Globe, like the Swan and other London theaters of the day, explains noted Shakespearean
scholar David Bevington,

> was essentially round, or polygonal, and open to the sky,
> forming an acting arena approximately 70 feet in diameter; [it]
> did not have a large curtain with which to open and close a
> scene, such as we see today in opera and some traditional the-
> ater. A platform measuring approximately 43 feet across and
> 27 feet deep . . . projected into the yard [central open area]. . . .
> The roof, above the stage and supported by two pillars, could
> contain machinery for ascents and descents, as were required
> in several of Shakespeare's late plays. . . . The underside of the
> stage roof, called the heavens, was usually richly decorated
> with symbolic figures of the sun, the moon, and the constella-
> tions. The platform stage stood at a height of 5 1/2 feet or so
> above the yard, providing room under the stage for under-
> worldly effects. A trapdoor . . . gave access to the space below.
> The structure at the back of the platform, known as the tiring
> house because it was the actors' attiring (dressing) space, fea-
> tured at least two doors. . . . [The Globe likely] also had a dis-
> covery space, or curtained recessed alcove, perhaps between
> the two doors—in which Falstaff could have hidden from the
> sheriff (in *Henry IV, Part 1*) or Polonius could have eaves-
> dropped on Hamlet and his mother. This discovery space
> probably gave the actors a means of access to and from the tir-
> ing house. . . . Scenery was not used, though the theater build-
> ing itself was handsome enough to invoke a feeling of order
> and hierarchy that lent itself to the splendor and pageantry
> onstage. Portable properties, such as thrones, stools, tables,
> and beds, could be carried or thrust on as needed.[16]

The audience, including the groundlings, those who stood in
the yard in front of the stage, generally watched the performances in afternoon. The best evidence suggests that the
Globe accommodated between two thousand and three thousand spectators in all. Between 1599 and 1607, its open-air pit
and arena stage were the scene of the premieres of most of
what are now viewed as Shakespeare's greatest tragedies.

These included *Hamlet, Othello, King Lear, Macbeth,* and *Antony and Cleopatra.*

Predating all of these masterpieces, and certainly worthy of being mentioned along with them, was *Julius Caesar,* one of the first plays ever presented at the new Globe Theatre. Most scholars accept that the play was composed in the summer and first performed sometime in the fall of 1599. The only surviving eyewitness account of this production is that of a Swiss doctor named Thomas Platter, who visited London that year and attended two plays, one of them *Caesar.* He later described the experience:

> After lunch on September 21st, at about two o'clock, I and my party crossed the river [the Thames], and there in the [play]house with the thatched roof [the Globe] we saw an excellent performance of the tragedy of the first Emperor Julius Caesar with about fifteen characters; after the play, according to their custom, they did a most elegant and curious dance, two dressed in men's clothes, and two in women's.[17]

Platter's reference to only fifteen "characters" almost certainly meant fifteen "actors." That the thirty-six characters (not counting extras) listed in the play's "Dramatis Personae" could be performed by so few players is explained by the fact that many actors commonly "doubled," or played two or more of the smaller roles in a single production. Platter's mention of the "curious dance" refers to a little jig that Elizabethan actors often performed as a kind of encore after the play was over.

About nine years after writing and producing *Julius Caesar,* Shakespeare began to devote less time to his profession and more to his family and community. Now secure in his fame and fortune, he seems to have increasingly retreated to his comfortable Stratford mansion, known as New Place, which he had purchased in the late 1590s. There, according to various entries in local records and diaries, Shakespeare involved himself in community affairs, at least partly in the distinguished capacity of a Stratford town councillor. Although he still wrote plays, he no longer maintained the breakneck pace of his youth. *Coriolanus, Pericles, The Winter's Tale, Henry VIII,* and *The Two Noble Kinsmen,* were all written and performed between 1608 and 1613. It appears that Shakespeare became seriously ill in March 1616, for his will was executed on March 25 and he died about a month later. Most of his estate went to his wife, sister, and daughters, although he also left money, as his will states, "to my fellows [theatrical colleagues], John Heminge, Richard

Burbage, and Henry Condell," to buy mourning rings. The will also states, "I give and bequeath unto the poor of Stratford . . . ten pounds [a substantial sum at the time]." [18]

Condell and Heminge proved to be true friends. In 1623 they published the so-called First Folio, a collection of the playwright's complete plays, under the title *Mr. William Shakespeare's Comedies, Histories, & Tragedies. Published According to the True Original Copies.* The First Folio was extremely important to posterity because it included eighteen of Shakespeare's plays that had not already been printed and that might otherwise have been lost forever. One of them was his great political play *Julius Caesar.* This work, along with *Macbeth, Hamlet, The Tempest, Antony and Cleopatra,* and Shakespeare's other incomparable theatrical pieces, literary scholar Harry Levin writes, have been

> accorded a place in our culture above and beyond their topmost place in our literature. They have been virtually canonized as humanistic scriptures, the tested residue of pragmatic wisdom, a general collection of quotable texts and usable examples. Reprinted, reedited, commented upon, and translated into most languages, they have preempted more space on the library shelves than the books of—or about—any other author. Meanwhile, they have become a staple of the school and college curricula, as well as the happiest of hunting grounds for scholars and critics. [19]

That *Julius Caesar* has been presented in many diverse settings and styles, with varying thematic emphases and character interpretations, is, of course, a testament to the universality of Shakespeare's writing. The play's enduring popularity also stems from the continuing interest in the real Julius Caesar as a man, soldier, politician, and dictator. It is likely that he will always remain an archetype, a symbol and prime example of ambitious politicians and would-be dictators, both of whom, we can be sure, will always lurk in the corridors of state power. Because the play *Julius Caesar* captures and explores this universal human archetype so masterfully, the names of Shakespeare and Caesar will undoubtedly be forever linked.

NOTES

1. Act 1, scene 1, lines 37–42.
2. Singly, each of the three lacked the power and resources needed to challenge the Senate successfully; by combining their wealth and influence, they could conceivably manipulate the government to their own ends.

3. Act 2, scene 2, lines 32–37.
4. Suetonius, *Julius Caesar*, in *Lives of the Twelve Caesars*, published as *The Twelve Caesars*, trans. Robert Graves, rev. Michael Grant. New York: Penguin Books, 1979, p. 28.
5. Act 1, scene 2, lines 115–118.
6. Suetonius, *Caesar*, in *The Twelve Caesars*, pp. 50–51. The remark, "You, too, my child?"—which Shakespeare later rendered as "Et tu, Brute?"—was a reference to the distinct possibility that Brutus was actually Caesar's son. At about the time that Brutus was born, Caesar had been his mother's lover.
7. Act 3, scene 2, lines 189–192.
8. For the sake of brevity and dramatic effect, Shakespeare combined the two battles into one decisive confrontation.
9. Appian, *Roman History*, trans. Horace White. Cambridge, MA: Harvard University Press, 1964, p. 353.
10. Octavian had earlier placed Lepidus under house arrest, effectively removing him from the Triumvirate.
11. Act 5, scene 3, lines 44–46.
12. Karl J. Holzknecht, *The Backgrounds of Shakespeare's Plays*. New York: American Book, 1950, pp. 33–34.
13. The date of his christening is registered as April 26, 1564. Since it was then customary to baptize an infant no later than the first Sunday or holy day following its birth, most scholars favor April 22 or 23 as Shakespeare's birth date. April 23 is also the day on which the English observe St. George's Day, a popular holiday. Regarding the end of Shakespeare's life, the date of his burial is known—April 25, 1616; and when the burial customs of the time are considered, April 23 seems a likely date for his death.
14. Quoted in Harry Levin, *The Riverside Shakespeare*. Boston: Houghton Mifflin, 1974, p. 4.
15. There is not a shred of proof to substantiate the legend that he left Stratford for London to escape prosecution for poaching (illegally killing deer and other game).
16. David Bevington, ed., *Julius Caesar*. New York: Bantam Books, 1988, pp. xxxii–xxxiii.
17. Quoted in Norman Sanders, ed., *Julius Caesar*. New York: Penguin Books, 1967, p. 7.
18. Quoted in François Laroque, *The Age of Shakespeare*. New York: Harry N. Abrams, 1993, p. 134.
19. Levin, *The Riverside Shakespeare*, p. 1.

CHAPTER 1

The Plot, Sources, and Setting of *Julius Caesar*

READINGS ON
JULIUS CAESAR

The Story Told in *Julius Caesar*

Marchette Chute

This concise but comprehensive summary of the plot of Shakespeare's great political play is by Marchette Chute, widely recognized as one of the twentieth century's leading authorities on English literary history. Chute helps bring her synopsis to life by working in some of the play's key and most famous lines and speeches.

Julius Caesar is a story of politics. It tells of treachery and good intentions and the manipulations of mass emotions, and it rises to the final tragedy of civil war. Shakespeare has taken a page of Roman history and used it to show some disastrous truths about the nature of men and politics, and the result is a masterpiece. . . .

The story opens in Rome, in the days when Julius Caesar was at the height of his political career, unquestioned master of the city and ruler of most of the known world. He is so much loved by the citizens that they decide to take "a holiday to see Caesar and to rejoice in his triumph," and two of the Roman officials are forced to disperse the cobblers and carpenters who have gathered in the streets to cheer him. For the politicians do not trust the enormous popularity of Julius Caesar. They are afraid he will become too confident of his own power and grow tyrannical in his use of it.

The scene shifts to a public square. Caesar is on his way to the races, with his public officials around him and an adoring crowd following, when someone shouts a warning: "Beware the ides of March." It is March already, and the ides fall on the fifteenth of the month. This is the first shadow of coming disaster, given by a man skilled in reading the future, but Caesar ignores it. "He is a dreamer; let us leave him; pass."

From *Stories from Shakespeare*, by Marchette Chute. Copyright © 1956 by E.P. Dutton. Copyright renewed 1984 by Marchette Chute. Reprinted by permission of Elizabeth Hauser.

BRUTUS AND CASSIUS

The crowd moves onward, and two men are left behind. One of them is Brutus, a noble Roman of an ancient family which has seen long service with the state, and the other is a brilliant politician named Cassius. Cassius has a plan in his mind—the destruction of Caesar—and he begins very delicately, to edge Brutus in that direction.

Cassius and Brutus are both old friends of Caesar, and Cassius begins to talk of the days when all three men were equal. He remembers particularly the time that Caesar challenged him to a swimming match and then would have drowned if Cassius had not rescued him.

>   And this man
> Is now become a god, and Cassius is
> A wretched creature and must bend his body,
> If Caesar carelessly but nod at him.

Cassius also recalls the time Caesar was sick of a fever in Spain, how he cried for water like a sick girl, and how he shook. "'Tis true, this god did shake." He is still an ordinary man, as he was then, but his political triumphs have exalted him into something almost beyond human control.

The wind brings a shout from the people at the races and Brutus remarks that he believes some new honor is being given Caesar. Cassius seizes the opening.

> Why, man, he doth bestride the narrow world
> Like a Colossus; and we petty men
> Walk under his huge legs . . .
> Now, in the names of all the gods at once,
> Upon what meat doth this our Caesar feed,
> That he is grown so great? . . .

Rome has always had a tradition of democratic government, and Cassius reminds Brutus it was one of his own ancestors who destroyed a tyrant and helped to found republican Rome. But Brutus will not commit himself, beyond a cautious promise to think over what Cassius has said.

They can speak together no longer, for Caesar is returning from the games. He eyes the gaunt fanatical Cassius, for the control of men is his business, and turns to his close friend, Mark Antony.

> Let me have men about me that are fat,
> Sleek-headed men and such as sleep o' nights:
> Yond Cassius has a lean and hungry look,
> He thinks too much: such men are dangerous.

Mark Antony refuses to believe that any danger can come
from a man like Cassius, but Caesar knows better.

> Such men as he be never at heart's ease,
> Whiles they behold a greater than themselves,
> And therefore are they very dangerous.
> I rather tell thee what is to be feared
> Than what I fear; for always I am Caesar.

Caesar in his own mind is above any such ordinary human
emotion as fear, for he is beginning to think he is as godlike
as the people believe him to be. The god is then obliged to
ask Mark Antony to walk at his right side rather than his left,
for he is deaf in his left ear.

A friend of Brutus named Casca has attended the games,
and Brutus, remembering the shouting, asks him what happened to Caesar there today. "Why, there was a crown offered him . . . He put it by with the back of his hand, thus:
and then the people fell a-shouting." Three times he was offered a royal crown and three times he refused it, although
in Casca's opinion he longed to possess it and only turned it
down to please the people. Finally, Caesar had them all in
such a state that they would have shouted for him if he had
"stabbed their mothers." "There was more foolery yet, if I
could remember it," says Casca, and goes home.

Brutus is shaken in his mind, and Cassius is sure that he
has caught him. For Cassius is planning nothing less than
the assassination of Julius Caesar, and he needs Brutus on
his side if the plot is to be a success. Now that his friend's
mind has begun to move in the right direction, Cassius decides to apply a little more pressure. He arranges for some
faked propaganda—petitions thrown into Brutus' window in
several kinds of handwriting so that it will look like a spon-
taneous outpouring of appeals from the citizens of Rome.

PLOTTING CAESAR'S "SACRIFICE"

There is a great storm that night with unnatural lightning
blazing in the streets of Rome and wild beasts walking in the
Capitol. It is a night full of portent, frightening to men who
believe in the supernatural; and Cassius, walking alone, is
able to use even the storm for his purposes. He encounters
Casca, compares Caesar to the storm and persuades Casca to
join the conspiracy.

Brutus has not been able to sleep that night. The talk he
had with Cassius has stirred up all the doubts and mistrusts

of Caesar that have been slowly developing in his mind, and
it has stirred also his profound, selfless devotion to Rome.
His family has always served the city, and the tradition is
bred in his bones. He cannot let a tyrant destroy his beloved
Rome; better to destroy the tyrant instead. But there is no
way to destroy the tyrant except by killing him, and Caesar
is his friend.

Brutus is roaming restlessly in his orchard when the
scene opens, and he sends his serving boy, Lucius, to light a
taper [candle] in his study. Then he turns to the problem that
has been haunting him all night and goes abruptly to the
heart of it.

It must be by his death.

Yet how can Caesar's death be morally justified, since he has
not yet committed any act of actual tyranny? Brutus has
great need to be sure of his moral position, since he is a good
man, and he argues with himself that anything is justified if
it prevents a future wrong. His boy Lucius brings him the
petitions he found lying by the open study window, and Brutus reads what he believes to be a call for help from the citizens of Rome. His ancestor destroyed Tarquin because he
was a tyrant; it is the equal duty of his descendant to destroy
Caesar.

Still, it is the murder of a friend that Brutus is contem-
plating, and he has a sense of being trapped in a dreadful,
hypnotic, downward pull that leads toward something from
which there is no return.

Between the acting of a dreadful thing
And the first motion, all the interim is
Like a phantasma, or a hideous dream . . .

Lucius comes to say there are men at the door, with hats
pulled down over their eyes and faces hidden in their cloaks,
and Brutus knows they are the conspirators, come to plot
murder. He lets them in.

The conspirators do not know if Brutus is one of them,
and they maintain an atmosphere of pleasant social inter-
course until Cassius is able to take Brutus aside and question him. Then he takes their hands once more, not as a
courteous host this time but as a fellow conspirator.

Brutus is determined that their deed shall not be thought
of as murder. It is a sacrifice, reluctant but unavoidable, and
he only wishes there were some way to kill Caesar's tyranny

without also killing Caesar. Since there is not, he is resolved to go through the whole action with a high Roman dignity, and from the first his ideas run counter to those of Cassius. Cassius, as a practical politician, wants them all to take an oath so that there can be no backsliding; but Brutus is convinced that no true Roman needs a formal oath to keep him in the path of duty. Cassius wants Mark Antony to be killed at the same time as Caesar, knowing quite well how dangerous he will be if he is left alive; but Brutus will not permit the thought of further bloodshed since they are "sacrificers not butchers."

"Cowards Die Many Times"

The act of assassination will be committed that day, the fifteenth of March at the eighth hour, and one of the conspirators promises to make sure that Caesar will be at the Capitol. By this time it is almost dawn and the men leave. The wife of Brutus sees them go, for she has been waiting to come in to her husband. She has been frightened by his restlessness and his inability to sleep, and since she is the daughter of a Roman statesman she knows how to approach him. In the end, Brutus promises to tell her what has been troubling him, for she has his trust and his love and is very worthy of both.

Caesar also has to deal with a frightened wife. The thunder and lightning have disturbed her sleep and she is fearful of natural omens. She tries to persuade Caesar not to go to the Capitol that day, since she is convinced his life is in danger, but he refuses to hide his head at home.

> Cowards die many times before their deaths,
> The valiant never taste of death but once.
> Of all the wonders that I yet have heard,
> It seems to me most strange that men should fear,
> Seeing that death, a necessary end,
> Will come when it will come.

She finally makes a direct appeal to him, asking him to stay at home for her sake, and Caesar agrees. Then one of the conspirators enters to play upon his vanity and on the idea of yielding weakly to a woman, and Caesar agrees to go to the Capitol.

On the streets leading to the Capitol, two people are waiting. One is a learned man, a teacher, who has found out about the conspiracy and has written on a piece of paper the names of the ringleaders. Caesar will pass that way, and the teacher hopes to fling the paper in his path as he comes along. Also waiting is the wife of Brutus, who knows what her husband intends to do that day and wants Lucius to go to the Capitol for news. She tries to be cheerful and calm, but her nerves are frayed almost to the point of agony. She is convinced she hears sounds from the Capitol until she learns that Caesar has not yet arrived, and then she is afraid she has let slip some word of her husband's intention. She sends the boy off at last to the Capitol, with pitifully vague instructions, and then goes indoors to wait. For there is nothing else she can do. She is only a woman, and politics belong to men.

THE ASSASSINATION

Caesar passes by along the street, and the learned man urgently tries to give him the list of conspirators. Caesar thinks it is one more petition and rejects it. He enters the Capitol, and one of the conspirators approaches him with a request to let a banished brother return to Rome. Caesar sees himself as one whose decrees are always just and therefore cannot be repealed.

> If thou dost bend, and pray, and fawn for him,
> I spurn thee like a cur out of my way.
> Know, Caesar doth not wrong, nor without cause
> Will he be satisfied.

All the conspirators kneel to him, begging him to grant the request, and Caesar scorns them all. "Hence! Wilt thou lift up Olympus?"

But Caesar is not the mountain of Olympus, nor is he a god. He is only a man and therefore mortal. The men who have surrounded him pull out their swords and stab him, and Caesar sees his friend Brutus among them. He gives the anguished cry—"And thou, Brutus?"—which Shakespeare left in the original Latin because everyone in the audience knew it already. "*Et tu, Brute?* Then fall, Caesar!" He falls dead at the base of Pompey's statue—Pompey whom he had defeated and destroyed—killed in his turn by the men who had been his friends.

One of the conspirators lifts up his voice in the cry that has been used to justify violence in all ages: "Liberty! Freedom! Tyranny is dead!" And Cassius declares with pride that they will be called "the men that gave their country liberty."

Instead, the gift is civil war, and the first seeds of it begin to grow almost at once. Mark Antony enters, the friend of Caesar whom Cassius had wanted to kill until he was overruled by Brutus. Mark Antony finds himself in a difficult position, obliged to smile on Caesar's murderers while he works out in secret his revenge. He asks the right to deliver the funeral oration over Caesar's body and Brutus gives it to him, in spite of the protests of Cassius. Cassius is an experienced politician, and he knows how easily a mob can be swayed by skillful oratory. But Brutus has great faith in reason. He is sure that if he explains carefully to the people of Rome what the motive was for the assassination and if he binds Mark Antony not to attack the good intentions of the assassins, everyone will understand the situation just as clearly as he does and there will be peace and freedom everywhere.

ANTONY SWAYS THE MOB

Brutus delivers an earnest speech to the people, carefully worded and as reasonable as the man himself. Then he leaves the citizens of Rome to listen to Mark Antony, and by doing so sets the seal of his own destruction. For Mark Antony is a great orator and a brilliant politician, and he plays on the emotions of the people with almost uncanny skill.

Mark Antony begins his speech faced by two difficulties. He is aware that the people are well disposed toward Brutus and he is also aware that he has promised to say nothing against the conspirators. Brutus has been able to convince the people that the conspirators acted only to save Rome, and they are so unwilling to hear any praise of Caesar that Mark Antony has to shout to make himself heard.

Friends, Romans, countrymen, lend me your ears!
I come to bury Caesar, not to praise him.

Beginning on that note, Mark Antony has their attention; and then, with diabolical precision, he begins to work toward the end he has in view. He says, and continues to say, that "Brutus is an honourable man," but little by little he begins to lead his hearers around to the point where they refuse to believe it. There is a low mutter in the crowd, a spark catching here and there, and Mark Antony tends the fire of their growing rage until it begins to crackle and roar.

Brutus has murdered their beloved Caesar, the godlike man who loved them so, and suddenly the fire sweeps through them as though they were dry grass. "Revenge! About! Seek! Burn! Fire! Kill! Slay!"

The mob surges through the city of Rome, looking for conspirators to kill, and finds a man who has the same name as one of the assassins. There is nothing else wrong with him, for he is the most harmless of poets, but since he has the same name there is clearly some kind of guilt by association. He cries out pitifully, "I am Cinna the poet, I am Cinna the poet. . . . I am not Cinna the conspirator." But he is torn to pieces.

The same brutality, but more calculating and coldblooded, is shown by the men who now control Rome. Mark Antony has formed a coalition with Caesar's grandnephew, Octavius, and with a colorless individual named Lepidus who is willing to carry out orders. The three men plan the destruction of everyone they do not trust, including some of their own relatives, and in the end they murder more than seventy of the senators of Rome. Then they set an army in motion to destroy Brutus and Cassius, although Mark Antony never had any illusions about the viciousness of civil war.

> Blood and destruction shall be so in use,
> And dreaful objects so familiar,
> That mothers shall but smile when they behold
> Their infants quartered with the hands of war . . .
> And Caesar's spirit, ranging for revenge,
> With Até by his side come hot from hell,
> Shall in these confines with a monarch's voice
> Cry 'Havoc!' and let slip the dogs of war . . .

CAESAR'S GHOST

Their enemies, Brutus and Cassius, are each at the head of an army, and Brutus has set up his camp near Sardis in Asia Minor. The two men love each other, but they have wholly different ideas about running the war. Cassius chooses the practical way, even if it should involve occasional financial dishonesty, and Brutus chooses the honorable one. His nerves are rubbed raw in any case, for he has just received the news that his wife has killed herself. She could no longer endure the strain of his absence and the fear of what Mark Antony might do.

Cassius comes to Sardis to bring his disagreement with Brutus out into the open, and there is the famous scene of two highly-wrought men, intelligent and loving friends, quarreling with each other like a pair of children. "I denied you not." "You did." "I did not." They make up with each other finally, but Cassius has seen a side of Brutus he did not know he possessed. "I did not think you could have been so angry." Brutus tells him of the death of his wife, and Cassius is honestly surprised at his own survival. "How 'scaped I killing when I crossed you so?" He wants to talk of the dead woman but Brutus cannot bear to have the subject mentioned, and they fall to a military discussion instead.

Again they cannot agree. Cassius wants to keep their forces where they are and wait for the enemy, and Brutus wants to march forth and meet them at Philippi [in northern Greece].

> There is a tide in the affairs of men
> Which taken at the flood leads on to fortune;
> Omitted, all the voyage of their life
> Is bound in shallows and in miseries.
> On such a full sea are we now afloat,
> And we must take the current when it serves,
> Or lose our ventures.

Cassius gives in, and the meeting is adjourned; for it is very late.

Brutus finds it difficult to compose himself for sleep, and when Lucius tries to soothe him with music the weary child falls asleep over the instrument. Brutus will not wake him, so he turns to a book he has been keeping in the pocket of his gown and starts reading.

The light flickers suddenly, and Brutus can read no longer. He lifts his eyes from the book, and the ghost of Caesar is standing in front of him. He does not recognize the apparition—"Speak to me what thou art"—and the ghost answers: "Thy evil spirit, Brutus. . . . Thou shalt see me at Philippi." He is trying to question the spirit when it vanishes. Lucius stirs in his sleep for he thinks he is still playing his instrument. "The strings, my lord, are false." More is out of tune than the strings of a musical instrument, for nothing now can keep Brutus from the battlefield and his destruction.

THE NOBLEST ROMAN OF THEM ALL

On the plains of Philippi there is a parley between the leaders of the two opposing forces, but it ends in insults. There is no escaping the coming battle, but Cassius faces it with a sense of foreboding, for birds of prey have been following as though looking for dead men. He and Brutus leave each other to command their two armies, and Brutus bids his friend farewell.

> This same day
> Must end that work the ides of March begun;
> And whether we shall meet again I know not. . . .

The battle swings back and forth, fiercely fought and fiercely in doubt, and in the confusion Cassius misunderstands what has happened. He thinks the enemy has conquered, and he is determined not to be brought back to Rome a captive. Brutus finds his friend at the foot of the hill, dead with his own sword in his heart, and the same sense of foreboding falls on Brutus in his turn.

> O Julius Caesar! thou art mighty yet!
> Thy spirit walks abroad and turns our swords . . .

The battle continues into the night, and one after another the friends of Brutus die. The remnant gathers itself together at a rock, and Brutus knows that the time has come to follow Cassius. He asks one of his servants to hold the sword steady, and he runs upon it and dies. His last words are addressed to an earlier and dearer friend than Cassius: "Caesar, now be still."

Mark Antony, the victor, looks down on the dead body of his foe and cannot find it in his heart to hate him. No one could hate a man like Brutus, who meant so well and was so tragically mistaken.

> This was the noblest Roman of them all.
> All the conspirators, save only he,
> Did what they did in envy of great Caesar;
> He only, in a general honest thought
> And common good to all, made one of them.
> His life was gentle, and the elements
> So mixed in him that Nature might stand up
> And say to all the world, 'This was a man!'

The Heart of the Plot: An Unnatural Conspiracy

Norman Sanders

At the heart of the plot of *Julius Caesar* lies the infamous conspiracy to assassinate the title character. This illuminating examination of the conspiracy is by Norman Sanders, a former professor of English at the University of Tennessee and highly respected Shakespearean scholar. Sanders first concentrates on the key scene near the play's opening, in which Cassius attempts to win Brutus over to the idea of killing Caesar by taking advantage of Brutus's trusting nature. Next, Sanders discusses Brutus's tragic mistake of believing rumors and innuendoes over solid proof of Caesar's tyranny. As Sanders points out, this is not the only way in which Shakespeare shows the conspiracy to be wrong-headed and doomed to ultimate failure. Monstrous omens, especially during a frightening storm, appear to taint the assassination plan as somehow unnatural. And subsequent scenes cast doubt on the justification of the conspirators' attempts to rationalize the murder as just or even as a necessary religious purification of a Rome threatened by the disease of tyranny.

To group Brutus and Cassius together merely as 'conspirators' or 'enemies of Caesar' is to oversimplify the nature of the conspiracy, because they are different in character, motive, and intention. For Cassius, the drive to murder Caesar is deeply written into his very nature. . . . As an 'unharmonious' man 'who loves no music', Cassius is branded as a figure of disorder on both the personal and political levels. Personally, his hatred of Caesar is grounded in envy at beholding a greater than himself; and politically, his abhorrence is based on his belief in a free, republican Rome whose wide walls should encompass more than a single

Excerpted from the Introduction, by Norman Sanders, to *Julius Caesar*, by William Shakespeare, edited by Norman Sanders. Copyright © 1967. Reprinted by permission of Penguin Books Ltd.

man. Neither of these emotions need necessarily lead a man to political action; but Cassius also has a philosophy that is more Renaissance than Roman, and which, to Shakespeare's original audience, was personified by the imperfectly-known but notorious figure of Nicolai Machiavelli [the notorious fifteenth-century Italian statesman who wrote about political power and manipulation]: this is the concept of man as master of his own destiny independent of any superhuman power:

> Men at some time are masters of their fates;
> The fault, dear Brutus, is not in our stars,
> But in ourselves, that me are underlings.

It is this combination of the hate-infested man and the convinced republican, who, in Plutarch's words, 'even from his cradle could not abide any manner of tyrants', who attempts to seduce Brutus to his party. As he does so, the two basic strains in his nature intertwine. On the one hand, he is totally sincere in his belief that he

> had as lief not be as live to be
> In awe of such a thing as I myself

because he was 'born as free as Caesar'. But he speaks of these beliefs in a context that devalues them. For he slips constantly from his high standards of republicanism into a more material and personal support of them. Caesar's pretensions certainly violate Cassius's ideals, but the physical limitations of Caesar in comparison with the personal standards Cassius sets are more immediately influential. Thus his own daring challenge of the elements and of Caesar is set against Caesar's weak response:

> Accoutrèd as I was, I plungèd in
> And bade him follow; so indeed he did.
> The torrent roared, and we did buffet it
> With lusty sinews, throwing it aside
> And stemming it with hearts of controversy.
> But ere we could arrive the point proposed,
> Caesar cried, 'Help me, Cassius, or I sink!'

It is this illustration that is brought forward to prove his point about individual freedom. Similarly, it is Caesar's fever in Spain which is used to show the human weaknesses of the eye 'whose bend doth awe the world', and of the tongue 'that bade the Romans / Mark him and write his speeches in their books'. In the Cassius who speaks of greatness in terms of feeding, and of honour in terms of personal achievement,

we have the man whose political grasp is limited to immediate practice, whose mind cannot grasp abstract concepts,
who can only perceive those standards which he himself
creates, and for whom politics is the realm of personal relationships in which he is naturally inept, yet in which he
craves success.

BRUTUS MANIPULATED BY CASSIUS

It is the function of this man to persuade Brutus, who is his
opposite in almost every respect, to join the conspiracy. Although, because of his egotism, he is unfitted for the role of
tempter, he is successful owing to the nature of the man he
tempts. For, though Brutus is able without effort to inspire
friendship and form close personal relationships, and has a
mind which moves easily in the world of ideals and abstractions, he is unable to 'look quite through the deeds of men'.
Throughout the scene between them, he is so wrapped in
his own thoughts and fears about Caesar that he only half-
listens to Cassius's words, or rather registers only those
among them that are directly connected with his own mis-
givings. Over-conscious of his own heritage and the historical associations of his name, he quickly responds to Cassius's calculated weighing of this name with Caesar's:

> Brutus and Caesar. What should be in that 'Caesar'?
> Why should that name be sounded more than yours?
> Write them together, yours is as fair a name;
> Sound them, it doth become the mouth as well;
> Weigh them, it is as heavy; conjure with 'em,
> 'Brutus' will start a spirit as soon as 'Caesar'.

With the sound of the crowd hailing Caesar offstage, he talks
to Cassius of his beliefs in generalizing, abstract terms not in
those of the immediate situation:

> If it be aught toward the general good,
> Set honour in one eye, and death i'th'other,
> And I will look on both indifferently. . . .
> Brutus had rather be a villager
> Than to repute himself a son of Rome
> Under these hard conditions as this time
> Is like to lay upon us.

It is due to these qualities in Brutus and to his fatal capacity for taking the name of a thing for the thing itself, or
the utterance of a principle as proof of its existence, that Cassius is able to twist his 'honourable mettle'. In Cassius's soliloquy at the end of Act I, scene 2, we have a clear if limited

statement of what we are to witness in the person of Brutus: namely, that qualities noble in themselves can be manipulated for less noble ends. In showing how he has used the friendship he longs for and himself professes to further a plan motivated primarily by personal envy, Cassius reveals the real nature of the conspiracy, which relies for its success on the conscious recognition that

> it is meet
> That noble minds keep ever with their likes;
> For who so firm that cannot be seduced? . . .

SUPPOSITION RATHER THAN PROOF

Despite the influence that Cassius can bring to bear on Brutus, both in personal encounter and by his device of planting forged letters purporting to represent the will of the Roman people, the decision which is to make the conspiracy a political fact rests with Brutus alone. It is for this reason that Shakespeare shows us only him in self-communication: for the decision must be seen to come out of his character. The speech recording this decision at the beginning of Act II is the crux of the play, and it has given rise to various and opposite interpretations. By this point, we are aware of what Brutus is, and, in the speech, all the tension between his nature and commitment to an action which violates this nature is obvious. Shakespeare is here trying to make credible simultaneously a man's determination to follow a course which, in terms of his character, is perverted, and those flaws and strengths in him which make such a perversion possible. But the degree of guilt we are meant to receive from the speech, and its implications for how we view Brutus, are variable. As the lines stand, Brutus misapplies logic wilfully, if unconsciously, and consequently decides on the basis of supposition and possibility, rather than on the proven evidence which points in the opposite direction. Although he admits that

> to speak truth of Caesar,
> I have not known when his affections swayed
> More than his reason . . .

yet he chooses to take the common proof over the particular instance and

> since the quarrel
> Will bear no colour for the thing he is,
> Fashion it thus: that what be is, augmented,
> Would run to these and these extremities;
> And therefore think him as a serpent's egg

Which, hatched, would, as his kind, grow mischievous,
And kill him in the shell.

MONSTROUS AND UNNATURAL HAPPENINGS

The degree to which one sympathizes with or blames Brutus at this moment depends upon one's over-all view of the play; but what is indisputable is that with Brutus's attempt to resolve, by whatever means, what is essentially a personal conflict with national implications, Shakespeare links other signs of disorder. The very words Brutus uses immediately following his moment of resolution convey the nature of the insurrection his whole being is undergoing, even as the state of Rome will as a result of it:

Between the acting of a dreadful thing
And the first motion, all the interim is
Like a phantasma or a hideous dream:
The genius and the mortal instruments
Are then in council; and the state of man,
Like to a little kingdom, suffers then
The nature of an insurrection.

This inward 'civil war' is that which is to produce its outward counterpart in the final scenes of the play; but it is also to have a more immediate correspondence in the warring elements and prodigies that are described by Casca in Act I, scene 3, and by Calphurnia in Act II, scene 2. These monstrous and unnatural happenings in the natural world were easily related by the Elizabethans both to man's inner life and to society itself, owing to the infinite series of interlocking correspondences which they perceived between the personal, social, material, and universal levels of life. For Casca,

When these prodigies
Do so conjointly meet, let not men say,
'These are their reasons, they are natural';
For, I believe, they are portentous things
Unto the climate that they point upon.

Cassius on the other hand sees it as a 'very pleasing night to honest men' which projects his own disordered state, and presents him with a challenge to test the will of the gods by placing himself 'even in the aim and very flash' of the 'cross blue lightning'.

How one interprets these phenomena in the play is in accordance with one's point of view; as Cicero rightly notes,

men may construe things after their fashion,
Clean from the purpose of the things themselves.

These unnatural happenings are connected with Caesar, and the disorder his tyranny creates in the body politic; but they also reflect the unnatural nature of the conspiracy against him, because 'The heavens themselves blaze forth the death of princes'. Both interpretations are voiced in the play, and Shakespeare pointed clearly to neither as being the right one. The final decision on this, as on so many other issues in the play, lies somewhere between Antony's laudation of Brutus and Brutus's own final lines on the futility of his action, between Caesar the man and Caesar the spirit.

THE ASSASSINATION A RELIGIOUS CEREMONY?

Once Brutus has made the conspiracy possible by joining it, Shakespeare focuses on Brutus's recognition of the unpleasant aspects of the undertaking to which he is committed, and on his efforts to bring those things he perceives into line with the exalted motives he believes to be prompting him. In meeting his fellow conspirators as they skulk into his house muffled in their cloaks in the dead of night, he defines the nature of what he has decided to do:

> O conspiracy,
> Sham'st thou to show thy dangerous brow by night,
> When evils are most free? O then, by day
> Where wilt thou find a cavern dark enough
> To mask thy monstrous visage?

As they confer at Brutus's house, the uneasy alliance of different personalities which the conspiracy really is begins also to emerge. What has been seen, up to this point, to be a balanced combination of the emotional drive and practicality of Cassius, and the necessary idealism of Brutus, turns out to have its own tensions. The price that Cassius has to pay for the plot's success is agreement to all of Brutus's errors of policy. The oath he proposes to bind them together is dismissed with an idealistic tirade by Brutus; and his advocacy of the need for Antony's death, as well as Caesar's, is denied as being butchery introduced into a sacrifice. Both of these decisions certainly grow out of those qualities which made Brutus's part in the conspiracy a necessity; but, more than this, they are a product of a Brutus who is now unconsciously trying to fit the violent means of the deed into his exalted vision of what the end will achieve. Thus an oath cannot be allowed, because they must not stain

The even virtue of our enterprise,
Nor th'insuppressive mettle of our spirits,
To think that or our cause or our performance
Did need an oath; when every drop of blood
That every Roman bears, and nobly bears,
Is guilty of a several bastardy,
If he do break the smallest particle
Of any promise that hath passed from him.

And Antony's death would introduce a sacrilegious note into what he visualizes as a religious ceremony in which the body must suffer for the spirit's sake:

Let us be sacrificers, but not butchers, Caius.
We all stand up against the spirit of Caesar,
And in the spirit of men there is no blood.
O, that we then could come by Caesar's spirit,
And not dismember Caesar! But, alas,
Caesar must bleed for it. And, gentle friends,
Let's kill him boldly, but not wrathfully;
Let's carve him as a dish fit for the gods,
Not hew him as a carcass fit for hounds.

THE CONSPIRACY SICK AND DIRECTIONLESS?

During the course of this scene, Brutus's image has been tarnished to some degree. Each member of the audience must perceive the distance between Brutus's vision and the actuality of the deed he contemplates. And Shakespeare introduces two short encounters which, in part, elevate him to his early eminence above the other conspirators. In the first, Portia [Brutus's wife] serves to remind us of the cost of Brutus's decision and the degree to which it affects his whole being as she describes, from the knowledge of intimacy, the past weeks:

It will not let you eat, nor talk, nor sleep;
And could it work so much upon your shape,
As it hath much prevailed on your condition,
I should not know you Brutus.

In the second scene, Caius Ligarius rises from his sick bed at Brutus's bidding, and, conjured by the magic of his name, is ready to follow

To do I know not what; but it sufficeth
That Brutus leads me on.

Yet, even though both these exchanges bring sympathy for Brutus, since they show us the trust and friendship and the love and devotion he can command, they simultaneously remind us by suggestion of other qualities. For Portia echoes her husband's awareness of his position, in her own pride in being Cato's daughter and 'the woman that Lord Brutus took to wife'; and she reflects also his blurring of the necessity for physical violence and the proving an ideal, as she shows him the gash in her thigh, self-inflicted to test her constancy. With Caius Ligarius, too, sickness touches the conspiracy: Caesar must be 'made sick', so a sick man is healthy and will join the plot, if Brutus 'have in hand / Any exploit worthy the name of honour'. . . .

Before the murder has actually been committed, all other considerations and decisions made by the conspirators seem to be of subsidiary importance; but those actions they perform in its aftermath are of prime significance in their results. It is immediately after Caesar has died that the conspiracy displays a lack of direction. At this point, the supernatural disorder of the previous night is given a human and social counterpart in the description of the city where

> Men, wives, and children stare, cry out, and run,
> As it were doomsday.

Some of the group share this hysteria, as Cinna and Cassius call for 'Liberty, freedom, and enfranchisement' to be proclaimed through the streets and in the common pulpits. Only Brutus has the calm necessary to reassure the aged senator, Publius; and this calm is based on his ability to keep in the forefront of his mind the abstract concept that the deed represents: namely, that 'ambition's debt is paid'.

Shakespeare's Guide to Republican Rome: Plutarch's *Lives*

Albert Furtwangler

It is well-known that in writing *Julius Caesar* Shakespeare closely followed the biographies of Caesar
and Brutus composed by the first-century A.D. Greek
historian, Plutarch. In this essay, Albert Furtwangler,
a professor of English at Mount Allison University in
New Brunswick, Canada, begins with a description
of the setting in which Plutarch wrote. The ancient
historian was born in the reign of the Roman emperor Claudius, the third successor of Augustus, who
had in his youth been Octavian, Caesar's adopted
son. Next, Furtwangler provides an informative summary of Plutarch's aims in writing the *Parallel Lives,*
his best-known work. As Furtwangler comments, Sir
Thomas North's translation of Plutarch's work was
extremely popular in the late 1500s. And Shakespeare expected a large number of theater-goers to
have read it before attending his play. Furtwangler
then explains how Shakespeare emphasized
Plutarch's presentation of the character of Brutus.
This was a character fascinating in all ages—a
philosopher-soldier, a man with both the intellectual
capacity to reason what course was best for his
country and the physical courage to pursue that
course.

The assassination of Caesar remained a dramatic memory.
Whether it was a sensational murder, a unique act of tyran-
nicide, a pivotal moment of revolution, or a transformation
of a man into a god, it was a scene to arrest and fascinate
great numbers of people both immediately and long afterward.

There are evident reasons why this had to be so. The conspirators' express aim was to bring down the greatest man of their time for just cause. And Caesar was himself a consummate master of public impressions. What he wore, how he moved or was carried, whether he stood or sat, how he was placed in relation to others around him, all mattered and were noticed in the frequent ceremonies and political gatherings of Rome. This was public life without newspapers or other intermediaries between a hierarchy of leaders and a large public of citizens who watched their daily appearances and felt their effects. Any unofficial appeal to a public, such as circulating a notice or calling a rally, might easily be suppressed by authority. The assassins had to both strike and plainly justify their deed in the same public gesture. Accordingly, they surrounded Caesar in a public place. They acted under color of their office, as senators rising against him in the senate. They each took a stab, to show both their solidarity and their numerous individual judgments against him. As it happened, the senate meeting that day was in a building built by Pompey, in a chamber with Pompey's statue. They killed Caesar at its base, as if to undo his conquest over that predecessor. And they left the body as it fell, to signify its unworthiness for further regard. That this was not enough was soon proved by events. But this was action without words, calculated to leave a powerful impression and get an attentive hearing for later words of justification. And it was action that was overcome only by other action, by the ritual and display of a calculated funeral.

PLUTARCH'S TWO LAYERS OF TRADITION

The full drama of the event can therefore hardly be suggested by any single historical account. But fortunately for us and for Shakespeare, there was a source from antiquity which managed to give full play both to Caesar and to Brutus, and to the long sweep of history and law and fate in which their lives had meaning. This was the collection of parallel lives written by Plutarch of Chaeronea, a source that gave special color and dignity to the career of Brutus.

Shakespeare drew heavily on Sir Thomas North's English version of Plutarch in writing *Julius Caesar*, and his borrowings, paraphrases, and transformations have been thoroughly scrutinized over the years. . . . Shakespeare did not blush to borrow heavily; in many places he observes fine details from Plutarch and includes them, even though a casual observer of the play might barely notice. It seems that he expected many in his audience to have read Plutarch—and indeed North's version was a popular book, running through many editions in Shakespeare's time. Perhaps he felt bound to provide such touches, just as modern plays and films are obliged to satisfy viewers who have already read the book. Some of Shakespeare's scenes do not make complete sense without a familiar knowledge of Roman ways.

But reading Plutarch and Shakespeare side by side creates its own distortions, especially where passages from one are printed as footnotes to the other. Plutarch provides more than colorful details or necessary explanations about Brutus and Caesar. He also places their lives in an inviting pattern of historical writing and views them with his own ample, distanced, well-balanced judgments. His *Lives* deserve to be read for themselves, as many in Shakespeare's audience are sure to have read them. A reader should afford the leisure to take in each long story and see its place in Plutarch's ambitious compendium of anecdotal biographies.

Plutarch grew up in Greece, studied in Athens, and lived most of his life in a remote Greek city. Many incidental remarks in his works show that he cherished the memory of ancient Greece, its Platonic philosophy and its political freedom. But his city, Chaeronea, was the site of Alexander's decisive conquest of the Greek city-states. And Plutarch was born in the reign of Augustus's successor Claudius, long after the Roman Empire was solidly established—though he records stories from older relatives about the battle of Philippi and the Egyptian feasts of Antony and Cleopatra. Plutarch had friends in Rome, visited there, and held Roman citizenship. Perforce he had to feel two deep layers of tradition embedded in the world he knew. As a Roman in the age of Hadrian, he had to acknowledge that ancient Greece was a memory. But as a scholar still writing Greek in Chaeronea, he could also view the most illustrious Romans as successors to older heroes.

The title of North's translation reads, *The Lives of the noble Grecians and Romans, compared together by that grave learned Philosopher and Historiographer, Plutarch of Chaeronea.* Most of Plutarch's career was given to writing moral and philosophical works, dozens of them, later collected as his *Moralia.* It was late in life that he undertook his series of biographies. And so he brought to it a mind seasoned with age; stored with learning and odd information; and practiced in both research and meditation on human nature, history, and the fortunes of the great. He wrote the lives, he said, to provide moral instruction, to excite emulation for noble actions. "Virtue," he wrote in the *Life of Pericles,* "instantly produces by her actions a frame of mind in which the deed is admired and the doer rivalled at one and the same moment. . . . Nobility exercises an active attraction and immediately creates an active impulse, not merely forming an eye-witness's personality by imitation, but producing a settled moral choice from the simple historical knowledge of the action. This is why I have made up my mind to spend my time writing biographies."

In order to set virtue vividly before his readers Plutarch developed two important strategies. One was to select telling little details as well as narratives of famous doings. "For the noblest deeds do not always show men's virtues and vices," he wrote in the *Life of Alexander,* "but oftentimes a light occasion, a word, or some sport, makes men's natural dispositions and manners appear more plain than the famous battles won wherein are slain ten thousand men, or the great armies, or cities won by siege or assault." Plutarch's second major strategy was to assemble a large collection of eminent lives and present them in pairs, matching the careers of the greatest Greeks with those of the greatest Romans. To most of these pairs he appended a brief summary comparison, highlighting the most salient strengths of character. This large framework of the *Lives* may seem ingenious, or it may seem awkward and downright pedantic—a colossal monument to the compare-and-contrast assignment that plagued students even in ancient schools. But Plutarch's parallel structure is a crucial feature of the *Life of Brutus.* It makes Brutus stand out as a special kind of Roman.

TWO PHILOSOPHER-SOLDIERS

Altogether Plutarch wrote well over fifty lives; twenty-three pairs and a few single biographies survived and were available to Shakespeare in English. Among the ancient Romans, Brutus's *Life* takes its place with those of Pompey, Cato, Cicero, Caesar, and Mark Antony. Each *Life* has an integrity of its own and repeats some events in a different light. In composing *Julius Caesar,* Shakespeare drew material from the accounts of Caesar and Antony and so fleshed out the finer qualities of Brutus's adversaries, just as Plutarch had done long before. Furthermore, each of these Roman figures is matched with a noble Greek, to bring out a well-defined pattern. Caesar is paired with Alexander, another brilliant world conqueror. Antony is compared to Demetrius, another general with vices as enormous as his virtues. The counterpart to Brutus is Dion, the disciple of Plato who overthrew the Syracusan tyrant Dionysius.

Plutarch introduces Brutus and Dion as men who embodied Platonic philosophy and set it to work in the world.

> Methinks that neither the Grecians nor Romans have cause to complain of the Academy, sith [since] they be both alike praised of the same in this present book, in the which are contained the lives of Dion and Brutus. Of the which, the one of them having been very familiar with Plato himself, and the other from his childhood brought up in Plato's doctrine, they both (as it were) came out of one self schoolhouse, to attempt the greatest enterprises amongst men. And it is no marvel if they two were much like in many of their doings, proving that true which their schoolmaster Plato wrote of virtue—that to do any noble act in the government of the commonwealth which should be famous and of credit, authority and good fortune must both meet in one self person, joined with justice and wisdom.

Of course many of Plutarch's other heroes were philosophical, too. Cato was a Stoic who died for his principles. Caesar was a renowned intellectual. Alexander was the pupil and patron of Aristotle. Cicero and Demosthenes won victories by their oratory. But Dion and Brutus are here paired as unique: high-minded men who stood out among coarser allies in perilous times. These accounts show philosophy in action in the harsh and dangerous work of confronting tyrants. . . .

Brutus was . . . a man almost comically tolerated as a scholar among soldiers, in this case Pompey's forces when Brutus came among them "to be partaker of the danger" of Caesar's pursuit.

> It is reported that Pompey, being glad and wondering at his coming, when he saw him come to him he rose out of his chair and went and embraced him before them all, and used him as honourably as he could have done the noblest man that took his part. Brutus, being in Pompey's camp, did nothing but study all day long, except he were with Pompey, and not only the days before, but the self same day also before the great battle was fought in the fields of Pharsalia, where Pompey was overthrown. It was in the midst of summer, and the sun was

very hot, besides that the camp was lodged near unto marshes; and they that carried his tent tarried long before they came, whereupon, being very weary with travel, scant any meat came into his mouth at dinner-time. Furthermore, when others slept, or thought what would happen the morrow after, he fell to his book, and wrote all day long till night. . . .

Here is the site of battle. The sun is hot. The air is miasmal [heavy and putrid]. Brutus is underfed and weary from travel. Caesar's approach has everyone tensed for danger. But while others catch sleep while they can, here is Brutus wide awake making an abstract of universal history! Plutarch repeats this image to describe Brutus's habits when

---

PLUTARCH INTRODUCES BRUTUS

In this excerpt from his Life of Brutus, *a principal source for the play* Julius Caesar, *Plutarch tells how Brutus was descended from an earlier Brutus, a man highly revered by Romans in late republican times.*

Marcus Brutus was a descendant of that Junius Brutus in whose honour the ancient Romans erected a statue of bronze and placed it in the midst of their kings. They represented him with a drawn sword in his hand in memory of the courage and resolution he had shown in dethroning the Tarquins [a royal line that ruled Rome before the founding of the Republic]. But the first Brutus possessed a character as unyielding as a sword of tempered steel. A hard man by nature, his disposition had never been humanized by education, and so his anger against the tyrants could even drive him to the terrible extremity of killing his own sons for conspiring with them. By contrast, the Brutus who is the subject of this Life took pains to moderate his natural instincts by means of the culture and mental discipline which philosophy gives, while he also exerted himself to stir up the more placid and passive side of his character and force it into action, with the result that his temperament was almost ideally balanced to pursue a life of virtue. So we find that even those men who hated him most for his conspiracy against Julius Caesar were prepared to give the credit for any redeeming element in the murder to Brutus, while they blamed all that was unscrupulous about it upon Cassius, who, although a relative and a close friend of Brutus, was neither so simple in character nor so disinterested in his motives.

Ian Scott-Kilvert, trans., *Makers of Rome: Nine Lives by Plutarch.* New York: Penguin Books, 1965, p. 223.

he and Cassius were preparing to face their last battle. Others turned to their rest, but Brutus went back to his studies. "After he had slumbered a little after supper, he spent all the rest of the night in dispatching of his weightiest causes; and after he had taken order for them, if he had any leisure left him, he would read some book till the third watch of the night; at what time the captains, petty captains, and colonels did use to come to him."

Plutarch heightens this impression by making Cassius a harsh foil to the gentler Brutus. As we saw earlier, he claims that Brutus was drawn into Cassius's murderous conspiracy. Later he shows Brutus behaving kindly toward a difficult ally.

> Men reputed [Cassius] commonly to be very skilful in wars, but otherwise marvellous choleric and cruel, who sought to rule men by fear rather than with lenity; and on the other side he was too familiar with his friends and would jest too broadly with them. But Brutus in contrary manner, for his virtue and valiantness was well-beloved of the people and his own, esteemed of noblemen, and hated of no man, not so much as of his enemies; because he was a marvellous lowly and gentle person, noble minded, and would never be in any rage, nor carried away with pleasure and covetousness; but had ever an upright mind with him, and would never yield to any wrong or injustice, the which was the chiefest cause of his fame, of his rising, and of the good will that every man bare him; for they were all persuaded that his intent was good.

Yet these accounts do not imply that Dion and Brutus were fastidious, well-meaning pedants who had no business being in court or camp among treacherous men. Quite the contrary. Plutarch presents them as strong, daring, capable leaders. That is what makes them fascinating. They could devote themselves to philosophy and still be effective in politics. They came close to being the ideal Platonists, statesmen who could discipline their minds and prevail in trials of power.

THE LAST WORD IN REPUBLICAN ROME

In Plutarch's judgment, it was only very narrowly that Brutus failed. Until the last moments at Philippi he had victory within his grasp. If he had known of a naval victory over the fleets carrying his opponents' supplies, he might well have planned his battles differently. He might have defeated Octavian and Antony so sharply that no emperor ever came to be. In the course of this biography, Plutarch sees into all the major versions of Brutus's significance. He allows that he could be ruthless. He notes that civil wars could be worse than the rule of a dictator. He stresses Brutus's courage against tyranny. Yet in the end he joins a geopolitical and a theological view in one momentous sentence. "Howbeit the state of Rome (in my opinion) being now brought to that pass that it could no more abide to be governed by many lords but required one only absolute governor, God, to prevent Brutus that it should not come to his government, kept this victory from his knowledge, though indeed it came but a little too late." And the gods underscored this point by sending Caesar's ghost to Brutus on the eve of battle.

One further impression from Plutarch deserves to be mentioned for its effect on Shakespeare and the modern world. When the playwright took up North's translation he had to turn the pages of a large and heavy volume. The fifty lives in the 1579 edition run to over 1,100 pages in one great folio, a ponderous printed monument of the ancient world. It might seem that Plutarch included every worthy of Greece and Rome down to the establishment of the empire. And in the traditional order of the lives Dion and Brutus came last among those that are paired, Brutus last of all. Plutarch indicates elsewhere that these lives were not the last to be written. But they were traditionally given the final place, so that Brutus followed Pompey, Caesar, Cicero, and Antony. Whether calculated or not, this arrangement gives Brutus the last word on republican Rome.

Contemporary Settings Illustrate the Play's Universality

Richard France

As written, the setting of Shakespeare's *Julius Caesar* is, of course, Rome in the first century B.C. Most often, stage and film productions have reproduced this setting, usually employing three-dimensional façades or painted backdrops of Roman buildings and dressing the characters in togas and other Roman garb. But though traditional and often effective, setting the story in ancient Rome is neither essential nor necessarily the most effective way to stage it. That the play's themes of political corruption and assassination are universal to almost all societies is demonstrated by the fact that some productions have successfully used modern settings. Perhaps the most famous and most often written-about example was the 1937 production of *Julius Caesar* directed by the legendary American stage and film personality Orson Welles.

In the 1930s and 1940s, Welles' talented group of actors and production people, collectively known as the Mercury Theater, became famous for their dramatic and often daring radio, stage, and film ventures. Welles' version of Shakespeare's *Caesar* is here described by Richard France, a noted playwright and veteran professor of Brown University and the University of Southern California. As France explains, Welles compared the republican crisis surrounding Caesar's dictatorship to the crisis the Western democracies faced in dealing with contemporary despots like Italy's Mussolini and Germany's Hitler. In doing so, France suggests, Welles showed that the story of Caesar's fall, as dramatized by Shakespeare, can reach out to and capture the imaginations of audiences, no matter in what age it is staged.

Rather than merely reviving Shakespeare's account of a tyrant's downfall in ancient Rome, Welles, in this the inaugural production of the Mercury Theatre, set about to arouse the passions of his audience with a simulation of the chaos then overtaking Europe. In doing so, he exploited their inevitable superstitions about dictatorships—so successfully, in fact, that more than one critic would proclaim that, in Welles's hands, *Julius Caesar* had about it "the immediate ring of today's headlines."

In the 1930s, the sight of fascist salutes and martial throngs, and the sound of demagogic ranting and angry mobs, had become a commonplace for anyone who listened to the radio or saw the newsreels or read such popular magazines as *Time* and *Newsweek*. Whatever else was not within their personal experience—such as stealth or conspiracy or gangsterism—had, in all probability, become familiar to the general public through their exposure to the movies. These were the sights and sounds that Welles employed as theatrical devices in *Julius Caesar*. For his audience, the production, which Welles subtitled "The Death of a Dictator," had the same immediacy as banner headlines that day after day proclaimed new and increasingly gruesome horrors being committed just across the Atlantic Ocean. "If the play ceases to be Shakespeare's tragedy," applauded one thunderstruck observer, "it does manage to become ours."

REVEALING THE PLAY'S ORIGINAL MEANING?

For him to properly exploit such emotional reverberations, however, Welles had to go beyond merely overlaying the outward appearances of contemporary catastrophe on a production in which they were plainly anachronistic [shown in the wrong time period]. Other updatings of Shakespeare, such as the W.P.A. production of *Coriolanus* the year before, had been received with disapprobation and ridicule. Welles needed a structure to carry his explosive symbols, and the one that best suited his purpose was melodrama.

His own working style quite naturally drew him to this genre, designed as it is for overdrawn characterizations, smashing climaxes, uncontrolled violence, and sentimental appeal. *Julius Caesar* included all of these. The frank theatricality that Welles used in fashioning his production as a political melodrama had both unity and coherence. Elements that otherwise would have seemed ridiculously overwrought were accepted as perfectly natural in the pervasive flamboyance of the melodramatic atmosphere from which they emerged.

Except for an occasional stage direction, none of the production's extreme theatricality was written into the text. . . . Those passages dealing with internecine [mutually destructive] rivalries were all but eliminated. By summarily cutting out most of the final two acts, Welles did away with the triumvirate and the ghost of Caesar.

Shakespeare begins his play with an encounter between two tribunes and members of the general public whose republican liberties it is the tribunes' duty to maintain. Rather than deal with the workings of the republic, Welles chose instead to open his production with Caesar's bravura entrance and the ominous warning from out of the darkness that accompanies it.

While shaping his text to emphasize the rapid flow of events, Welles did not wholly eliminate the complexities of Brutus as a man "with himself at war." Brutus voices his feelings about the necessity for stopping the ambitious Caesar and his repugnance against committing the slaughter. And while his lines were not reworked to give him proletarian sympathies, within the theatrical schema Brutus became identified with contemporary liberals. For more than one reviewer, this Roman aristocrat exemplified "the unhappy fate of the liberal in a world torn by strife between the extreme left and the extreme right."

Likewise, many who attributed the play's contemporary quality to Welles's direction were equally convinced that it was merely a matter of highlighting what were, in fact, Shakespeare's own political sensibilities. This led them to expound on his liberalism and hatred of dictatorships. Curiously overlooked, even by the left, was Shakespeare's fealty [loyalty] to that long succession of absolute monarchs, the Tudor line. . . .

Theatrical effects devised to make *Julius Caesar* seem contemporary were thus misunderstood as methods for extracting the *real* Shakespeare. Welles, "in the sharp design of his production, has caught the play's meaning [and] lifted an Elizabethan voice into the modern world of dictators to make a lusty shout of protest." Such judgments cannot be attributed simply to a particular critic's lack of historical grounding. In a majority of those reviewing this production, there appears to have been an overwhelming desire to believe that *Caesar*'s original meaning had, at long last, been revealed.

THE AUDIENCE SWEPT ALONG IN THE ACTION ONSTAGE

The production's foremost booster was John Mason Brown of the *New York Post*. . . . His exacting standards were notoriously hard to meet. When the Mercury company learned that Brown, after attending the final dress rehearsal, was enthralled and delighted by the production, they had good reason for optimism regarding its critical reception. In his review Brown was moved to hyperbole. "Orson Welles stages the tragedy magnificently in modern dress and makes it an unforgettable experience." His more serious judgment was that *Julius Caesar*, though ceasing to be Shakespeare's tragedy, became, instead, one which belonged to a modern audience. But even for Brown, the Mercury production best served to underscore Shakespeare's currency. "Mr. Welles proves in his production that Shakespeare was indeed not of an age but for all time."

Richard Watts echoed this sentiment. Noting how lackluster the theatre season had been, Watts was relieved to find in this *Julius Caesar* "something to stand up and cheer about." A major reason for his approbation was that "never once does it seem to you that anything new has been written into Shakespeare's *intent* (italics mine)." The production also led Watts to a revelation that he described almost wistfully: "You cannot escape the feeling that, with the clairvoyance of genius, [Shakespeare] was predicting for us the cauldron of modern Europe."

So enthralled were the Mercury audiences that even the most perceptive among them often lost sight of what was actually going on. [Noted critic] Euphemia Van Rensseler Wyatt revealed a precise awareness of the liberties that Welles had taken with Shakespeare's text. But when it came to the mob's encounter with Cinna the Poet, she too was swept along by the virulence and brutality that Welles had built into this brief scene.

> Not even the Group Theatre in all their frenzy against dictators ever divised a more thrilling scene than that in which the poet, Cinna, is swallowed up by an angry mob, and yet one comes home to find that Shakespeare wrote it just that way.

Possibly Wyatt . . . was pleased to believe that a faithful adaptation of Shakespeare could serve [a contemporary political] purpose. As Stark Young pointed out, however, Welles reordered this scene from Shakespeare's play (III, iii) more radically than any other in his production. "The scene in Shakespeare is short, and is partly comic relief. This Mercury version makes a long scene of it, writes in lines, puts in much business and turns it all into gripping sarcasm and horror."

Although it was clearly not Shakespeare's intention to make this short scene, which lacks any significant action and wherein none of the major characters of the play appears, the emotional high point of his play, that is what it became in Welles's hands. Stark Young described the aftermath of this climactic moment.

> We jump then to the quarrel scene of Brutus and Cassius. For the rest of the play is Brutus'—Brutus realizing his disaster, Brutus in a brief scene with his page, Brutus running on his sword, and over Brutus' body Antony's epilogue of praise.

At its most vital point, *Julius Caesar* dealt with the fate of a single man. To Norman Lloyd, who played Cinna, his character "symbolized what was happening in the world, if your name was Greenburg—and even if you weren't Jewish." The Mercury audience made Cinna's experience their own, representing as it did their worst fears for themselves and for those dearest to them abroad.

APPLYING A MODERN SPIRIT TO THE PLAY

Welles imposed upon himself strict limitations in adapting *Caesar* . . . and audiences, while delighting in his handling of the materials, also found their abiding conservatism satisfied with the knowledge that every word of text was, in fact, written by Shakespeare. Welles's own devotion to his favorite author would not have allowed him to do otherwise. . . .

In his assimilation of the modernist spirit, Welles became imbued with many of its formal devices, which he used to give such productions as *Julius Caesar* intellectual and emotive qualities that surpassed anything previously seen on the American stage. . . . As his production of *Julius Caesar* would demonstrate, Welles was able to extend such resources as he had at his command to their utmost, and to stretch the imaginative and aesthetic possibilities available to his audience.

CHAPTER 2

Brutus, the Pivotal Character

READINGS ON
JULIUS CAESAR

Shakespeare's Brutus: A Man Torn by Conflicting Values

J.L. Simmons

Brutus is usually acknowledged as the central character of Shakespeare's *Julius Caesar*. This is mainly because Brutus's moral dilemma about whether or not to
turn on his friend, Caesar, and join the conspiracy,
constitutes the play's dramatic core. This essay, by
Shakespearean scholar J.L. Simmons, author of *Shakespeare's Pagan World*, examines this dilemma by comparing two conceptions of Brutus's character. The first
is the one presented by Plutarch in his famous first-
century B.C. work, *Parallel Lives*, the main source of
Shakespeare's play; the second is Shakespeare's conception of the character in that play. As Simmons points
out, in Plutarch's view Brutus was justified in killing
Caesar. Plutarch's Brutus attempts to separate ideal
from reality by claiming that Caesar's death is a sacrifice for Rome's betterment, rather than a simple murder. Shakespeare, on the other hand, Simmons contends, saw in Plutarch's Brutus the potential for
showing a man torn by conflicting moral values. How,
for instance, could such a seemingly gentle and rational man take part in such a savage act as the assassination? According to Plutarch, the answer was that Brutus
put the good of his country above his friendship with
Caesar. For Shakespeare, however, this was not enough
in itself to account for Brutus's betrayal of Caesar. And
therein lies the play's high drama.

Sir Thomas North's translation of Plutarch's *Lives* gave
Shakespeare . . . the basis of characterization and event for
Julius Caesar. . . . Shakespeare gives coherence and purpose
to what must have appeared from his more encompassing

point of view to be unresolved contradictions. Plutarch's investigation of the assassination and its participants is far from simplistic; nevertheless, the biographer's ultimate approval of Brutus and his republican ideals finally brings about a political endorsement of his part in the conspiracy against Caesar. In the *Lives* . . . that endorsement leads to two rudimentary, though apparently unrecognized, paradoxes in which Shakespeare saw potentialities for tragedy as well as irony: (1) Plutarch sympathetically isolates his Brutus from the cruelty and violence of the assassination and from the morally impure motives of his fellow conspirators; (2) Plutarch affirms Brutus's honor and wisdom even though the killing of Caesar has no effect, other than deleterious [harmful], on Rome's political need for the rule of one man.

THE TWO SIDES OF BRUTUS'S NATURE

After noting that Brutus framed his mode of life and action "by the rules of vertue and study of Philosophy," a fact that accounts to a great extent for Plutarch's warm admiration, the biographer establishes the Roman's nobility by citing the approval given even by the supporters of Caesar: "So that his very enemies which wish him most hurt, because of his conspiracie against *Iulius Caesar:* if there were any noble attempt done in all this conspiracie, they referre it wholly vnto *Brutus,* and all the cruell and violent acts vnto *Cassius.*"

This isolation of Brutus from the central fact of violent murder on the basis of noble and unselfish motivation is almost totally complete in Plutarch. Shakespeare sees the irony of this impossible separation of ideal and reality, a separation revealed in Brutus's attempt to make the act a sacrificial rite transcending and thereby obscuring the reality. Not only must the ideal distract from the reality; the motivating heart must feign innocence of the action:

> And let our hearts, as subtle masters do,
> Stir up their servants to an act of rage,
> And after seem to chide 'em.

But just as the reality of murder cries out insistently after the deed, the ritual of blood accentuating rather than alleviating the fact of blood, so the act makes merely ironic the claim of a pitiful heart:

> Though now we must appear bloody and cruel,
> As by our hands and this our present act
> You see we do; yet see you but our hands,

And this the bleeding business they have done.
Our hearts you see not; they are pitiful. . . .

BRUTUS'S "GREAT MINDE"

Plutarch offers other hints that there is a moral and psychological dichotomy [division into two parts] in Brutus's nature. The account of Caesar's ambivalence towards Brutus defines these opposing forces: "Now *Caesar*... did not trust [Brutus] overmuch, nor was not without tales brought vnto him against him: howbeit he feared his great minde, authority, & friends. Yet on the other side also, he trusted his good nature, & fayre conditions." Perhaps the major differences between Shakespeare's and Plutarch's attitudes toward Brutus lies in their estimations of Brutus's "great minde." Plutarch seems to have unqualified admiration. Shakespeare recognizes potential irony in a "great minde" conflicting so violently with a "good nature."

Though this developing irony is gradual and sympathetic, Shakespeare's final comment, when Brutus and Cassius exchange views on suicide, is unmistakably critical. . . . Shakespeare emphasizes the philosophical inconsistency by not allowing a blind Brutus to acknowledge or even to recognize his own contradiction. The playwright chooses this moment of moral incoherence to echo North's laudatory phrase "great minde":

Cas.   If we do lose this battle, then is this
      The very last time we shall speak together.
      What are you then determined to do?
Bru.   Even by the rule of that philosophy
      By which I did blame Cato for the death
      Which he did give himself—I know not how,
      But I do find it cowardly and vile,
      For fear of what might fall, so to prevent
      The time of life—arming myself with patience
      To stay the providence of some high powers
      That govern us below.
Cas.   Then, if we lose this battle,
      You are contented to be led in triumph
      Thorough the streets of Rome?
Bru.   No, Cassius, no. Think not, thou noble Roman,
      That ever Brutus will go bound to Rome;
      He bears too great a mind.

If Caesar was right to fear Brutus's "great minde"—though the reason for its danger is not the same in Plutarch as in Shakespeare—there was justification for trust in his "good nature, & fayre conditions." Indeed, Shakespeare's basic dramatic problem in the material for his play must have been, rights and wrongs aside, how so gentle and good-natured a man could take part in so bloody an act. The answer for Plutarch is all to Brutus's credit: "*Brutus* preferr[ed] the respect of his country and common wealth, before priuate affection." For a large segment of critical opinion, this statement encompasses Brutus's tragedy. Certainly the material lends itself to a conflict between public and private affections; and Shakespeare makes use of that conflict. But for the core of *Julius Caesar* to lie here, the friendship between

---

BRUTUS TRIES TO JUSTIFY CAESAR'S MURDER

This is the section of Plutarch's Life of Brutus *in which, directly following the assassination, Brutus demands "strict justice" of the conspirators. Minutes later, Brutus tries to justify the deed to the Roman people, contending it was necessary for everyone's liberty; to his surprise, however, he receives a hostile reception.*

At last, when Caesar had been done to death, Brutus stepped into the midst of the debating chamber and did his best to reassure the senators and persuade them to stay. But they took to their heels in confusion and crowded panic-stricken through the doors, although nobody made any move to pursue them. For it had been firmly decided that one man and one only was to be killed, and the rest of the people were to be invited to take up their liberty. When they had discussed the execution of their plan, all the other conspirators had thought it necessary to kill Mark Antony as well as Caesar. They regarded him as a man who despised the law, favoured autocratic rule, and had acquired great power through his ability to mix familiarly with his soldiers and command their loyalty; and, lastly, his natural arrogance and ambition had become more dangerous than ever, because he had been raised to the dignity of the consulate and was at that time a colleague of Caesar. Brutus, however, opposed this idea. He insisted in the first place that they should act only with strict justice, and he also held out the hope that Antony might undergo a change of heart. He still cherished the idea that once Caesar was out of the way, Antony's generous nature, ambition, and love of glory would respond to the noble example set by the conspirators, and that he would join them in helping their country to achieve her liberty. In this way Brutus actually saved Antony's life, but in the general alarm which followed the murder, Antony put off his senator's toga, disguised himself in plebeian dress, and made his escape.

Brutus and Caesar would be central; and that friendship is not . . . dramatically rendered. To be sure, Shakespeare refers to the friendship and even assumes it; but he does not develop the tragedy of a man who for the welfare of his country kills his best friend. That is another, unwritten play. Shakespeare questions Plutarch's approval not because of the preference given to public over private virtues. . . . His ironic doubt is rather directed toward Plutarch's assumption that Brutus acted with wisdom in "respect of his country and common wealth."

Brutus and his companions then went up to the Capitol, and with their hands smeared with blood and brandishing their naked daggers, they called upon the citizens to assert their liberty. At first they were greeted only by cries of fear, and the general confusion was increased by people wildly running to and fro in the terror which followed the news of the assassination. But since there was no more bloodshed and no looting of property, the senators and many of the people took courage and went up to the conspirators in the Capitol. When a large crowd had assembled, Brutus made a speech which was calculated to suit the occasion and please the people. His audience applauded him loudly and called upon him to come down from the Capitol, and the conspirators, their confidence returning, now made their way to the Forum. The rest of them walked together, but Brutus found himself surrounded by many of the most distinguished men in Rome, who escorted him in their midst with great honour from the Capitol, and conducted him to the rostra. The crowd which faced him was an audience of mixed sympathies and had come prepared to raise a riot, but at the sight of Brutus it was overcome with awe and awaited his words in orderly silence. When he came forward to speak, they listened intently to what he said, but the moment that Cinna took his place, and began to denounce Caesar, it became clear that many of his listeners were far from pleased with what had been done. The crowd's anger began to rise, and they abused Cinna so violently that the conspirators were obliged to take refuge again in the Capitol. Thereupon Brutus sent away the most distinguished of the citizens who had accompanied him, as he was afraid that they might be besieged there, and he did not think it right that they should run such a risk, considering that they had no share in the deed.

Ian Scott-Kilvert, trans., *Makers of Rome: Nine Lives by Plutarch.* New York: Penguin Books, 1965, pp. 237–39.

SOMEONE MUST BE CAESAR

Creating disturbing moral ambiguities, Plutarch's second unexamined paradox reinforces Shakespeare's skepticism. Plutarch approves of Brutus despite a recognition that Rome of necessity must have an absolute ruler. Plutarch first indicates this inevitability when he comes to the civil war between Caesar and Pompey:

> The citie remain[ed] all that time without gouernment of Magistrate, like a ship left without a Pilote. Insomuch, as men of deepe iudgement & discretion seeing such furie and madnesse of the people, thought themselues happy if the common wealth were no worse troubled, then with the absolute state of a Monarchy & soueraign Lord to gouerne them. Furthermore, there were many that were not affrayed to speake it openly, that there was no other helpe to remedy the troubles of the common wealth, but by the authority of one man only, that should command them all.

After the overthrow of Pompey's sons in Spain, Rome reluctantly makes Caesar a perpetual dictator, but for a reason quite appealing to Tudor sensibilities:

> The Romaines inclining to *Caesars* prosperitie, and taking the bit in the mouth, supposing that to be ruled by one man alone, it would be a good meane for them to take breath a little, after so many troubles and miseries as they had abidden in these ciuill warres: they chose him perpetuall Dictator. This was a plaine tyranny: for to this absolute power of Dictator, they added this, neuer to be affraide to be deposed. . . .

The question that Plutarch does not face is how to reconcile Brutus's wisdom with his evident blindness regarding the nature and condition of the state. If "men of deepe judgement," not to mention God, see the necessity for an absolute ruler, on what grounds could a man whose life is directed by philosophy and whose main concern is for the good of Rome kill the obvious and even the de facto choice?

One can see in Shakespeare's source other considerations that, along with practical politics and providence, urge the necessity of one-man rule. Plutarch's exploration of the corrupt Roman Republic, where nearly everyone is ambitiously struggling for power or selfish gain, affords vivid evidence of a degeneracy that explains the need for a single authority. With the exception of Brutus, all the other participants in the event oppose Caesar not because of principle but because of envy. They want to be Caesar themselves:

All [were] perswaded that [Brutus's] intent was good. For they did not certainly beleeue, that if *Pompey* himself had ouercome *Caesar*, he would haue resigned his authoritie to the law: but rather they were of opinion, that he would still keepe the soueraigntie and absolute gouernment in his hands, taking onely, to please the people, the title of Consull or Dictator, or of some other more ciuill office. And as for *Cassius*, a hot, chollericke, & cruell man, that would oftentimes be caried away from justice for gaine: it was certainly thought that he made warre, and put himself into sundry dangers, more to haue absolute power and authorities then to defend the libertie of his country. For, they that will also consider others, that were elder men then they, as *Cinna, Marius,* and *Carbo:* it is out of doubt that the end & hope of their victorie, was to be Lords of their country: and in manner they did all confesse that they fought for the tyranny, and to be Lords of the Empire of Rome. And in contrary manner, his enemies themselues did neuer reproue *Brutus,* for any such change or desire.

It goes without saying that Antony and Octavius have the same desire "to be Lords of their country." There is either going to be perpetual civil war or someone is going to be Caesar, because the tendency and desire of everyone involved—except Brutus—is to rise to the top. . . .

NATURE'S LAW CANNOT BE DENIED

Another aspect of the nature of man that Shakespeare's world view could incorporate more easily than Plutarch's and that argued for the necessity of absolute rule stands in paradoxical opposition to carnal self-interest. In spite of all protests against submission, the people of Rome and even the conspirators look to a superior for a ruler. Plutarch sees it as "a wonderfull thing, that [the people of Rome] suffered all things subjects should doe by commaundement of their kings: and yet they could not abide the name of a king, detesting it as the vtter destruction of their liberty." This observation is taken from the "Life of Antonius," but Shakespeare follows the passage closely for Casca's report of Antony's offering Caesar the coronet. Shakespeare understands the ambivalence of the mob far better than Plutarch does, and in the play this irony flourishes. Whereas Plutarch shows the people to be incensed that Caesar returns triumphant after his victory in Spain, Shakespeare dramatizes a heroic welcome by these same former worshipers of Pompey. The mob has its reluctance to see Caesar pronounced king, but its instinct for hero-worship will not be denied. Ironically Caesar's refusal of the symbolic crown merely increases the mob's adulation. When Shakespeare in the central scene of the play has that voice shout to Brutus, "Let him be Caesar" (III.ii.50), the implicit is acknowledged.

Shakespeare's Brutus does not know this tendency in man or at least cannot grapple with its implications. He is, however, unwittingly the beneficiary of it, not only during his oration but within the conspiracy itself. In Plutarch the secret letters from the people are sent to Brutus by those "that desired chaunge, and wished *Brutus* onely their Prince and Gouernour aboue all other." In having Cassius forge these letters, Shakespeare makes a meaningful change to show Cassius's duplicity and Brutus's gullibility and to avoid suggesting the people's dissatisfaction with Caesar. Nevertheless, the play follows Plutarch in the conspirators' demand that Brutus be their leader: "Now when *Cassius* felt his friendes, and did stirre them vp against *Caesar:* they all agreed and promised to take part with him, so *Brutus* were the chiefe of their conspiracie." The suggestion that Brutus, to the consternation of Cassius, becomes a Caesar within the conspiracy would have startled Plutarch. Shakespeare develops the irony mercilessly, for the law of nature—not to mention that of God and of practicality—is not to be denied, whatever man's pretentions.

As a matter of fact, Plutarch must have seen this irony, if only momentarily as "a wonderfull thing." When Brutus and Cassius meet in Sardis, "there, both their armies being armed, they called them both Emperors." The translation is exact, though throughout the Middle Ages and the Renaissance there was frequently a semantic confusion between the military title *imperator* and its subsequent meaning, after Augustus adopted it, of absolute ruler. Plutarch continues immediately with the material that Shakespeare would focus into the crucial quarrel between Cassius and Brutus, the dissension that Plutarch recognized "commonly hapneth in great affaires betweene two persons, both of them hauing many friends"—between two "Emperors," in this case. Although the quarrel has no moral import for Plutarch, he does show another manifestation of this Caesar principle (if I may so designate it) when, before the battle, "*Brutus* praied *Cassius* he might haue the leading of the right wing." Significantly, Shakespeare transfers this detail to Antony and Octavius: since the quarrel scene states the theme sufficiently for the conspirators' side, Shakespeare now quickly hints that the principle is inevitably operating, in momentous anticipation of later history, within the other camp.

SHAKESPEARE HELPED TO RESOLVE PLUTARCH'S PARADOXES?

Two paradoxes, then, permeate the source material for *Julius Caesar*, but they are not developed or reconciled with Plutarch's fundamental approval of Brutus and disapproval of Caesar. . . .

The paradoxes and moral ambiguities come through clearly in Plutarch, especially when he is attempting absolute justification. That the jarring elements are not meaningfully resolved is no discredit to him. For Plutarch, Brutus's ideal was a practicable one: it had worked in the best times for Rome and Greece, and it might work again. If God finally helped to create a monarchy, it was not the result of the condition of man or the laws of nature but the necessities of a specific period of unfortunate degeneration exacerbated by a few particular men like Julius Caesar. Brutus's attempt proved futile, but it was nevertheless honorable. Except for a few tactical errors, the blame for his failure must rest entirely on the age.

The evidence in Plutarch worked for an altogether different synthesis in Shakespeare. The material of the source— Brutus's sympathetic and ideal vision struggling against the need for a Caesar and the nature of man—was comprehensible and reconcilable in terms not available to Plutarch. Shakespeare did not have Plutarch's vantage point for a complete endorsement of Brutus. But the Christian humanism of a later age offered a perspective that helped Shakespeare to create a coherent tragic experience out of the confusion and confinement of the historical moment.

Brutus's Personal Failure Is the Central Tragedy

Alice Shalvi

In this essay, Alice Shalvi, a distinguished Shakespearean scholar of Hebrew University of Jerusalem,
singles out Brutus as the tragic hero of *Julius Caesar*.
Brutus's honor, Shalvi maintains, is his central motivating force and it is his honorable regard for the
"general good" of the Roman people that leads him
to join the conspiracy against Caesar. Ironically,
though, it is that very sense of honor that ends up
unraveling the conspirators' plans for Rome. By allowing Antony to live and underestimating Antony's
own oratorical abilities and personal ambitions, Brutus fails to achieve his noble goal—the restoration of
Rome's republican system. And personal failure, says
Shalvi, is the central tragedy of the play. Shakespeare's message, she suggests, is that people must
act to fulfill their own individual destinies and not
allow themselves merely to be swept along by historical currents. Yet ironically, even when they take the
initiative, it does not always bring about the results
they desire.

The earliest of Shakespeare's mature tragedies, *Julius Caesar*
and *Hamlet*, both present a similar ideal in the characters of
their heroes, but they serve to illustrate what happens to the
noble man when he is placed in a situation which tests his
nobility to the uttermost and they show the tragic limitations
of nobility when it is confronted by really evil forces. . . .

Despite the title of the play, it is Brutus who is the tragic
hero of *Julius Caesar;* it is his fate which is the central concern of the play. Brutus's prime characteristic is his honour.
Descended of valiant ancestors who 'did from the streets of

From Alice Shalvi, "Shakespeare's 'High Roman Fashion': Julius Caesar," © 1967 by
Alice Shalvi, in *The World and Art of Shakespeare,* by A.A. Mendilow and Alice Shalvi
(Jerusalem: Israel Universities Press, 1967). Used by permission of Alice Shalvi.

Rome / The Tarquin drive when he was called a king', de-
rived from that Brutus who 'would have brooked / The eter-
nal Devil to keep his state in Rome / As easily as a king',
Marcus Brutus fears the threat to Rome's liberty which is
implied in Caesar's desire for kingship and autocratic rule.
Unlike Cassius, whose prime motivation is clearly a personal envy of Caesar, Brutus is wholly unselfish in his devotion to the welfare of the Roman Republic and prepared to
face even death if this is required for his country's good.
'What is it that you would impart to me?' he asks Cassius,
when the latter first broaches the subject of Caesar's ambition:

> If it be aught toward the general good,
> Set honour in one eye and death i' the other,
> And I will look on both indifferently,
> For let the gods so speed me as I love
> The name of honour more than I fear death.

BRUTUS'S NOBILITY MAKES HIM UNFIT

Brutus is the only one of the conspirators who is portrayed
as inwardly debating the justification for commiting the
'dreadful thing' which Cassius proposes, and once again
Shakespeare stresses that it is no personal animosity towards Caesar that motivates Brutus, but only a regard for
the 'general good'. The ultimate factor in persuading Brutus
to join the conspiracy is his belief that his countrymen wish
him to act on their behalf, a belief based on the letters cast
in at his window or conspicuously left for him in public
places. These letters we, however, know to come from the
wily Cassius, who realises that there is no other way to win
over an honourable man to commit an act of violence and
evil than by making him believe the act to be honourable.
The conspirators need Brutus precisely because he is known
to be honourable and will therefore lend colour to their conspiracy when the time comes to justify their action to the
people of Rome. As Casca says:

> . . . he sits high in all the people's hearts:
> And that which would appear offence in us,
> His countenance, like richest alchemy,
> Will change to virtue and to worthiness.

So we are shown how the man of virtue, with none but the
best of motives, may become the tool of men less noble than
himself. Cassius himself draws the correct conclusion:

Well, Brutus, thou art noble; yet, I see,
Thy honourable metal may be wrought
From that it is disposed: therefore it is meet
That noble minds keep ever with their likes;
For who so firm that cannot be seduced?

Yet, ironically, it is Brutus's nobility which in fact unfits him for the conspiracy and brings about the reversal of his noble aims. Inevitably, because of his greatness, Brutus becomes the leader of the conspirators and his essential goodness and moderation overrule the subtler perceptions of the wily Cassius. He refuses to permit Antony to be killed together with Caesar and, despite Cassius's arguments to the contrary, he permits Antony to make the funeral-oration over Caesar's body which rouses the populace against the conspirators. Secure in the knowledge that he has acted in all sincerity and for the good of his country, Brutus fails to take into account both Antony's Machiavellian wiles (which the equally Machiavellian Cassius *does* suspect) and the fickleness of the masses, who are like 'blocks and stones and worse than senseless things'. He makes the tactical errors of allowing Antony to have the last word, of leaving him alone with the crowd and of letting him produce the dead body of Caesar. The great difference between Brutus and Antony is excellently conveyed by the contrast between the monotonous rhythms of Brutus's prose and the impassioned, oratorical art of Antony, who skilfully uses the device of repetition with the recurrent phrase, 'honourable men'. There is no doubt which of them better understands the mentality of Rome's masses. It is Brutus's political ineptitude after the assassination and his military ineptitude in insisting on meeting the enemy at Philippi that bring about his own downfall and that of Cassius, and the ineptitude stems primarily from essential innocence, naïveté and goodness. . . . Shakespeare here stresses that goodness is not sufficient qualification for the dirty business of politics, indeed that it virtually disables a man from fulfilling the tasks of leadership.

CAESAR'S VANITY

But it is not alone Brutus's ineptitude that brings about the reversal of the conspirators' hopes and plans. The real cause of the defeat of Brutus lies in the fact that the murder of Caesar is an act of evil, an act of horror, that has to be expiated. Politically, the overthrow of Caesar may be necessary for the welfare of Rome. This is brought out by the way in which Caesar is portrayed. He is a great warrior, who, in the past, has done good service for his country but he returns to Rome now having triumphed over no alien power but over Pompey, the great Roman general. Caesar is vain and conceited. Infirm in body, deaf in one ear and subject to epileptic fits, fearful of attack from men such as Cassius who 'think too much', Caesar nevertheless believes himself 'immortal' and aspires to be king of Rome. He grows angry when the crowd cheer his repeated rejection of the coronet offered him by Mark Antony instead of urging him to accept it. The people's tribunes are put to death for 'pulling scarves off Caesar's images' and, when Calpurnia's prophetic dreams and the augurers' warnings dissuade him from venturing forth on the Ides of March, Caesar camouflages his fears with an imperious message to the senators, whom he contemptuously dismisses as 'greybeards':

> Decius, go tell them Caesar will not come.
> . . . .
> The cause is in my will: I will not come;
> That is enough to satisfy the senate.

Like most conceited men, Caesar is susceptible to flattery and yet prides himself on being immune to it. As Decius says: 'When I tell him he hates flatterers, / He says he does, being then most flattered'. It is by appealing to Caesar's vanity and ambition that Decius persuades him to reject the counsels of Calpurnia and the soothsayers, for he tells Caesar that this is the day on which the senators mean to offer him the crown and that they may well change their minds if he fails to appear. Arrived at the Senate, Caesar further reveals his weaknesses of character. Once again he prides himself on immunity to flattery as he rejects the supplications of Metellus Cimber:

> . . . Be not fond,
> To think that Caesar bears such rebel blood
> That will be thaw'd from the true quality
> With that which melteth fools; I mean, sweet words,
> Low-crooked court'sies and base spaniel-fawning.
> Thy brother by decree is banished:
> If thou dost bend and pray and fawn for him,
> I spurn thee like a cur out of my way.
> Know, Caesar doth not wrong, nor without cause
> Will he be satisfied.

As supplicant after supplicant kneels before him to urge the repeal of Publius Cimber's banishment, Caesar remains firm

in his sentence, and speaks of himself in terms which indi-
cate clearly that he thinks of himself as a demi-god:

> . . . I am constant as the northern star,
> Of whose true-fix'd and resting quality
> There is no fellow in the firmament.
> The skies are painted with unnumber'd sparks,
> They are all fire and every one doth shine,
> But there's but one in all doth hold his place:
> So in the world; 'tis furnish'd well with men,
> And men are flesh and blood, and apprehensive;
> Yet in the number I do know but one
> That unassailable holds on his rank,
> Unshaked of motion: and that I am he.

How ironic these assertions of steadfastness are in the light of
the previous scene in which we saw him vacillating between
the conflicting advice of Calpurnia and Decius. What Caesar is
being so adamant about is in refusing pardon and mercy, the
truly god-like qualities in man. It is the moment of his downfall: his unyielding pride and vanity lead to his death.

MURDER MUST BE AVENGED

Thus Shakespeare makes it clear that Brutus's fears are justified. It is apparent that Caesar in power would bring servi-
tude to Rome, and, if the only way to prevent Caesar from at-
taining power is by murdering him, the murder is
presumably justified. Nevertheless, the murder is never
wholly condoned by Shakespeare. Brutus speaks of it be-
forehand as a 'dreadful thing' and it is important to note his
uncertainty as to Caesar's tyranny; the outcome of crowning
Caesar is left deliberately uncertain: 'So Caesar *may:* / Then
lest he may, prevent'. The murder itself is shown onstage in
its full brutality and violence, with the out-numbered Caesar
helplessly overwhelmed by his enemies, and almost immediately after the murder our feelings are swayed in favour of
Caesar by Antony's genuine mourning and the terms of
praise in which he refers to the dead man: 'Thou art the
ruins of the noblest man / That ever lived in the tide of
times'. Brutus's treachery in participating in the murder is
particularly stressed, since it is his presence among the assassins which so appals Caesar as to make him cry out the
famous 'Et tu, Brute? Then fall, Caesar!' And after the murder we have the strange appeal of Brutus to his colleagues to
stoop and bathe their hands in Caesar's blood and then proceed with their blood-besmeared swords to cry 'Peace, free-

dom and liberty' in the market-place. This serves as an ironic counter to his earlier remonstrances:

> Let's kill him boldly, but not wrathfully;
> Let's carve him as a dish fit for the gods,
> Not hew him as a carcass fit for hounds:
> And let our hearts, as subtle masters do,
> Stir up their servants to an act of rage,
> And after seem to chide 'em . . .

Indeed, the corruption in Brutus has, inevitably, set in earlier, since it was essential for him, together with the other conspirators, to pretend a friendliness towards Caesar which none of them really felt. Brutus is aware of this terrible hypocrisy, for his reaction on seeing the masked conspirators arriving at his house in the night is:

> . . . O conspiracy,
> Shamest thou to show thy dangerous brow by night,
> When evils are most free? O, then by day
> Where wilt thou find a cavern dark enough
> To mask thy monstrous visage? Seek none, conspiracy;
> Hide it in smiles and affability:
> For if thou hath, thy native semblance on,
> Not Erebus itself were dim enough
> To hide thee from prevention.

Yet he himself later bids them

> . . . look fresh and merrily;
> Let not our looks put on our purposes,
> But bear it as our Roman actors do,
> With untired spirits and formal constancy.

Shakespeare implicitly condemns the conspiracy, then, on two scores: firstly, because it inevitably involves moral corruption even in the best and noblest of men and, secondly, because murder is always, no matter in what circumstances or however it may be justified, bloody and cruel. 'Blood' is the word that echoes and re-echoes throughout the scenes which follow the assassination—and blood will have blood. Murder must be avenged and Caesar does indeed achieve vengeance. Though his ghost appears physically only once, in visitation upon Brutus before the battle of Philippi, Caesar's presence broods over the action after his murder just as much, if not more, than it did during his life-time. 'He doth bestride the narrow world like a Colossus' and his influence does not end with his death. Antony, at the close of Act III, sc. i, utters a terrible prophecy which ends with what is, in effect, an invocation of Caesar's ghost:

Woe to the hand that shed this costly blood!
Over thy wounds now do I prophesy,—
Which, like dumb mouths, do ope their ruby lips,
To beg the voice and utterance of my tongue—
A curse shall light upon the limbs of men;
Domestic fury and fierce civil strife
Shall cumber all the parts of Italy;
Blood and destruction shall be so in use
And dreadful objects so familiar
That mothers shall but smile when they behold
Their infants quarter'd with the hands of war;
All pity choked with custom of fell deeds:
And Caesar's spirit, ranging for revenge,
With Até by his side come hot from hell,
Shall in these confines with a monarch's voice
Cry 'Havoc,' and let slip the dogs of war;
That this foul deed shall smell above the earth
With carrion men, groaning for burial.

The prophecy is most horribly fulfilled and Caesar has his revenge on the men who murdered him.

"CAESAR, THOU ART MIGHTY YET!"

The revenge takes various forms. Firstly, we learn of Brutus and Cassius's desperate flight from the vengeful mob, a flight from the very city they had sought to free from tyranny and for which Brutus, at least, had been prepared to lay down his life. Then we see the dissension which develops between these two men, leading to insult, accusation and open quarrel in IV, iii. We may note the way in which the assassination is referred to here, when Brutus warns Cassius of the consequences of corruption:

Remember March, the ides of March remember:
Did not great Julius bleed for justice' sake?
What villain touch'd his body, that did stab,
And not for justice? . . .

There is irony here in the fact that Brutus still believes that the murder was commited for wholly noble ends and has still not seen through the essentially corrupt and self-centred motives of the other conspirators.

Later in the same scene we learn of the death of Portia, Brutus's wife, and this, too, is indirectly the outcome of the assassination, for, Brutus says,

Impatient of my absence,
And grief that young Octavius with Mark Antony
Have made themselves so strong: . . .
. . . with this she fell distract,
And, her attendants absent, swallow'd fire.

The ghost of Caesar calls himself 'Brutus's evil spirit'; he is unseen by any of the other people present and may . . . be interpreted as an emanation of the murderer's guilty conscience. He warns Brutus that he will see him at Philippi and although the ghost never reappears it is indeed the assassination which is once again the central theme referred to by the leaders on both sides during the parley that precedes the battle. Octavius warns his opponents that the battle will not end 'till Caesar's three and thirty wounds / Be well avenged; or till another Caesar / Have added slaughter to the sword of traitors'. The two sides join battle, Cassius's tents are set on fire and he sends his good friend Titinius to ascertain whether the nearby troops are friends or enemies. By a tragic error, he is deceived into believing them enemies, into believing himself responsible for his friend's death and into thinking capture imminent. He takes the truly noble way out: he kills himself—with the same sword as he had used in killing Caesar. His last words are significant: 'Caesar, thou art revenged, Even with the sword that killed thee'. And equally significant is young Cato's comment on Cassius's death: 'O Julius Caesar, thou art mighty yet! / Thy spirit walks abroad, and turns our swords / In our own proper entrails'. The same point is made again at the close of the play, when Brutus's dying words as he kills himself are 'Caesar, now be still, / I killed not thee with half so good a will'. With the death of Brutus the crime is finally expiated and Caesar's ghost may rest at ease. Vengeance has been achieved.

But to show that blood will have blood and that murder will be avenged is not Shakespeare's main purpose in this play. It is not simply a revenge tragedy in the Senecan tradition so popular in Elizabethan England. The consequences of the murder of Caesar are not confined to his murderers, for perhaps the most tragic result of the assassination lies in Brutus's failure to achieve by this act of violence the original, noble goal for which he had committed the crime. He had, as we have seen, one sole justification for killing his friend: Caesar's death was demanded by the 'common good', the general welfare and prosperity and freedom of the Roman people and the Roman Republic. What we are shown is that an act may lead to the very reverse of what the committer of the act intended and bring about precisely what it aimed at preventing. The immediate result of the assassination is Mark Antony's successful oratorical exploitation of the assassination and the hacked body to arouse the ignorant, fickle Roman mob against the

conspirators. Antony cares nothing for the 'common good'. He
seeks vengeance for his friend's death and power for himself.
This is clear from the coldly callous comment as the mob goes
off in fury: 'Mischief, thou art afoot, / Take thou what course
thou wilt'. The course it takes is the most terrible one of irrational, bloodthirsty violence. In the very next scene we witness
the lynching of Cinna the poet, torn to pieces despite his desperate avowals that he is not Cinna the conspirator: 'Tear him
to pieces for his bad verses . . . Pluck but his name out of his
heart, and turn him going . . . Tear him, tear him'. This wild,
unrestrained, bloodthirsty mob-rule finds an icy counter-point
in Act IV, sc. i, the scene that immediately follows it. What has
been the outcome for Roman government of Caesar's assassination? Who is in power *now?* Three dictators instead of one.
The opening words of the first scene in which we witness the
new triumvirate at work are ominous: 'These many then shall
die, their names are prick'd'. The cold-bloodedness is stressed
by the equanimity with which Lepidus and Antony barter a
brother's death for that of a nephew:

> ANTONY: These many, then, shall die; their names are prick'd.
> OCTAVIUS: Your brother too must die; consent you, Lepidus?
> LEPIDUS: I do consent,—
> OCTAVIUS: Prick him down, Antony.
> Upon condition Publius shall not live,
> Who is your sister's son, Mark Antony.
> ANTONY: He shall not live; look, with a spot I damn him.

And Antony's cold, calculating hypocrisy is proved by the
contempt with which he speaks of 'old Lepidus' and plots to
get rid of him once Lepidus has served his own and Octavius's purpose.

It is to this, then, that Brutus's act of salvation has brought
Rome and it is now that we can appreciate the full irony of that
cry of 'Liberty, Freedom and Justice' which succeeded the assassination. The country is divided in civil war, its government
in the hands of men as ruthless as Caesar and probably far less
honest and valiant than he was—men who, in injustice, will not
fall short of what Caesar would have been even had he become
king. Brutus's aims are, therefore, tragically reversed; it is for
this that he has betrayed friendship and committed a crime.

Nevertheless, despite the tragic reversal of Brutus's aims and
the vision of Rome governed by ruthlessly cruel men, the play
concludes with a re-affirmation of the dignity of man and the
worthwhileness of human life and this re-affirmation is to be

found in the essential nobility of Brutus, which is re-asserted and confirmed in the final scenes of the play that show his suffering and defeat. Similarly, Cassius is now displayed as possessing a nobility of character which had not been revealed earlier in the play. Both men accept their fate with truly noble Roman stoicism. 'No man bears sorrow better' we are told of Brutus's response to Portia's death, and the same noble acceptance of fate is typical of him and of Cassius before and during the final battle at Philippi.

Acceptance of fate's decrees does not, however, mean passivity and inaction on the part of the individual. Brutus is no Romeo, bemoaning the way in which Fate overrules his plans and hopes. The key words in this play, spoken by Brutus and indicating what is now Shakespeare's view of the respective rôles of Destiny and Free Will, are:

> There is a tide in the affairs of men,
> Which, taken at the flood, leads on to fortune;
> Omitted, all the voyage of their life
> Is bound in shallows and in miseries.
> On such a full sea are we now afloat;
> And we must take the current when it serves,
> Or lose our ventures.

This is an echo of Cassius's earlier words: 'The fault, dear Brutus, is not in our stars, / But in ourselves that we are underlings'. Our destiny lies in ourselves, is dependent on the way we seize the opportunities given to us by chance or fate or destiny or whatever name we choose to give to the superior force which exists in the universe.

Thus both Brutus and Cassius, enlightened as to the cause of their downfall, aware of their guilt in murdering Caesar, take the painful, courageous way of suicide rather than allowing themselves to be led as captives through the streets of Rome. . . . We feel the truth of Brutus's dying assertion:

> I shall have glory by this losing day
> More than Octavius and Mark Antony
> By this vile conquest shall attain unto.

The important thing here, as in all tragedy, is not physical triumph and survival, but self-conquest, the exorcism of all that is weak, ignoble and vilely human in the hero's nature, so that he goes to his death purified and spiritually triumphant over the forces that oppose him.

Courage and endurance are the two important qualities which Brutus proves himself to possess. His plans may have gone tragically awry and, what is more, the very act which he committed may have been shown by Shakespeare to have been evil. Nevertheless his crime is counterbalanced by the magnificent way in which he expiates it, by the suffering which it causes him. This suffering ennobles Brutus, it ennobles his fellow-conspirator, Cassius, its spectacle ennobles the audience and, most significantly, it impresses his enemies. It is Mark Antony who delivers the valedictory oration and correctly describes Brutus as 'the noblest Roman of them all'. Antony is aware that:

> All the conspirators save only he
> Did that they did in envy of great Caesar;
> He only in a general honest thought
> And common good to all, made one of them.
> His life was gentle, and the elements
> So mix'd in him that Nature might stand up
> And say to all the world 'This was a man!'

This is a fitting summary of the way in which Brutus has been portrayed throughout the play: a truly gentle, noble, man, kind to his servants, loving to his wife, slow to anger and speedily pacified, honest and generous. He makes one tragic error: he believes a crime to be justified when the aim is a noble one. This is fiercely negated by Shakespeare who here, as in the history-plays, shows that nothing justifies murder. But Shakespeare presents no satisfactory alternative solution to the problem of the just, honourable man living in a time of vice and corruption, other than to imply that if one engages in political combat one must be utterly ruthless and discard all thoughts of mercy and moderation. Had Brutus heeded Cassius and slain Antony all might have been well—except that Brutus would have shown himself even more corrupt and evil. Shakespeare here shows us the tragic dilemma of the good man called upon to combat evil and stresses that it is impossible to fight evil without becoming corrupted oneself. The tragic dilemma of Brutus is also the tragic dilemma of Hamlet. In this, the earlier of the two plays, no solution is offered to the dilemma. However firm a reassertion Shakespeare here makes, through the character of Brutus, of man's essential nobility and his capacity for spiritual greatness in the face of physical defeat, politically the play ends on a note of pessimistic query.

Without a Strong Brutus, the Play Founders

Roger Manvell

The role of Brutus is absolutely central to Shakespeare's *Julius Caesar*. In fact, says Roger Manvell,
former head of the Department of Film History at the
London Film School and director of the British Film
Institute, Brutus's character constitutes the play's
"center of gravity." The other characters, no matter
how important in their own rights, Manvell maintains, "must be seen in their relationship to, or effect
upon, this central figure . . . a reluctant conspirator"
who agrees to kill Caesar "only because he feels it is
for the ultimate good of Rome." Thus, says Manvell,
a substandard performance of Brutus's role can spell
failure for any production of the play. Manvell sub-
stantiates this point in the following excerpt from his
highly regarded book, *Shakespeare and the Film*. He
singles out the film version of *Julius Caesar* released
in 1970 by producer Peter Snell and director Stuart
Burge, a production that starred Charlton Heston as
Antony, John Gielgud as Caesar, and Jason Robards
as Brutus. Robards brought entirely the wrong acting
style to the role, Manvell contends. As a result, the
film lost its center of gravity and did not measure up
to the very well-received 1953 MGM movie, which
starred Marlon Brando as Antony, James Mason as
Brutus, John Gielgud as Cassius, and Louis Calhern
as Caesar.

In 1967, the Canadian producer Peter Snell, with only the
documentary *Royal Ballet* and the filmed theatre production
of *The Winter's Tale* behind him, started his preparation for
making another version of *Julius Caesar* in Britain for Com-

Reprinted from chapter 7 of *Shakespeare and the Film*, by Roger Manvell (New York:
A.S. Barnes). Copyright © 1971, 1979 by Roger Manvell. Endnotes in the original have
been omitted here.

monwealth United [Studios]. An initial impetus was given to this production when Charlton Heston, who had a great desire to play Antony again, agreed to do so for the phenomenally low fee of $100,000, plus 15 per cent of the world gross the film might earn. With his box-office seemingly secure with the presence of this star, Peter Snell added Sir John Gielgud to the cast to give the film that other necessity, prestige. The director chosen was Stuart Burge, who had directed the film of the National Theatre's production of *Othello,* with Laurence Olivier [in the mid-1960s]. . . . The total budget finally agreed was $1,600,000, one of the lowest in recent times for a film which involved the spectacular use of crowds, and battle scenes which had to be shot on location in Spain.

FRESH INTERPRETATIONS OF ANTONY AND CAESAR

It was not until 1969 that Peter Snell finally assembled his cast—the seemingly disparate group of men who had to weld themselves together as a production team, highly conscious of the previous version by Mankiewicz, which haunted them like some unlaid ghost. They were determined to achieve something quite different. Heston wanted to play Antony as a sensual, power-seeking opportunist. During the two-week rehearsal period in London he developed the idea of Antony swaying the crowd in the Forum scene by arguing with them individually at first and so gradually gaining his ascendancy over them as a whole, inciting them to riot. He stood on top of the rostrum steps, the crowd far below him and the great columns of the Forum set towering over him. 'Now let it work,' etc., he claimed, should then be taken as a separate scene immediately following, while Antony drinks wine. Things can take their course. Played in this style, Heston's volatile Antony is in marked contrast to Brando's stolid thug. John Gielgud's Caesar would of necessity be different from that of Louis Calhern. The new Caesar is urbane, and even witty, his ascendancy due to a natural feeling of social and intellectual superiority to the lesser men about him in the Senate. He respects only Brutus, whom he never actually confronts in the play until the final moment of death. Gielgud insisted on retaining many lines originally cut in the script; they must be kept for the sake of rhythm, he claimed, and won his point. He knew the play far better than any of them, and found it difficult to remember the cuts. 'You must not truncate the natural cadences of Shakespeare—nor the content,' he is reported as saying. How often such truncating takes place on the stage, and especially in the films of Shakespeare's plays, so that the organic flow of the verse is entirely lost!

BRUTUS'S INNER STRENGTH

The most exacting problem of interpretation lies always with Brutus, a part James Mason had underplayed in the 1953 version. Robert Vaughn (who plays Casca so effectively) is said to have wanted it; Peter Snell (unaccountably) is said to have wanted Omar Sharif; Orson Welles, approached for Casca, asked for Brutus, but disappeared from the cast altogether in the final stages. So Jason Robards, who had never even seen *Julius Caesar* performed, became Brutus, and determined to give the part a new, untraditional and modern slant—a man troubled by the morality of political assassination. He did not like the rehearsals Burge called prior to the shooting period, and disappeared. He wanted to capture Brutus's dilemmas before the camera, not in the rehearsal room.

The character of Brutus is the key to the play, its centre of gravity. All the other characters, important though they may be in their own right—as Caesar, Cassius, Antony, Casca and Octavius undoubtedly are—must be seen in their relationship to, or effect upon, this central figure, this stoic philosopher, a reluctant conspirator who accepts the necessity for violence against his friend, Caesar, only because he feels it is for the ultimate good of Rome. Any production without a strongly orientated personality playing Brutus will founder, leaving the centre of the stage to what are really only the secondary, though more 'showy' characters of Caesar, Antony and Cassius. The actor who plays Brutus cannot be 'showy'; he must establish his central position to the play through his display of an inner strength which outshines the more rhetorical strength of the showmen. This is what the play is about, and it needs an actor of the calibre (and experience in Shakespeare) of a Paul Scofield [the renowned British actor and Oscar-winner] to make this apparent at every instant in the action—he must radiate his point of view (mistaken or otherwise) throughout the total length of the play, dominating the conspiracy once he is drawn into it. That he fails, because he functions above the level of mere opportunism and unscrupulousness which guide the power-politicians on both sides, is the measure of the tragedy in the play. It is the reason for his comparative failure in dealing with the crowds in the Forum, not from any inability to sway them momentarily by the weight of reason (Shakespeare gives him a highly rational speech in prose to deliver, and the crowd responds to it), but because he does not realize that in loosing Antony to them he is selling them to the devil and the rule of unreason. But, for the play's sake, Brutus must be acted throughout from strength; the primary part to cast, therefore, is not Antony (the old actor-manager's dream because of its egocentric showmanship), but Brutus. And it was in the casting of Brutus that the film foundered.

A Brutus Who Lacks Stature

Jason Robards is an actor of considerable personality, and his approach to the part had a serious, if perhaps over-contemporary slant pitched well below the level of the character. The very naturalism he imposed on the delivery of the verse robs Brutus of the august power which he should increasingly reveal as the action develops. Robards brings to the part the worried intensity of [the American journalist famous for his investigative news pieces] Edward R. Murrow (whom he closely resembles) in his famous telecasts exposing Senator McCarthy. His Brutus is undoubtedly a good man, but he is not a great one. This largeness of nature must emerge in the two significant scenes between Brutus and Cassius; in the first, Cassius, the able opportunist, uses his debating skill to work on the great man's conscience, and in the second, he vents his barely controlled rage against the almost priggish coldness and aloofness of Brutus when he, too, feels his stoic calm giving way to anger. In the second of these scenes Robards quarrels as hotly as Cassius, and the whole point of the contrast between these men is lost. In the first, he merely appears worried. Although he obviously brings thought to the part, he gives it no stature. So once again, the central character goes by default, and the audience is left with the histrionics to carry the film through—Charlton Heston's splendid Forum scenes, for example, or the excellently choreographed assassination of Caesar, in the Senate, with man after man going in for the kill until, when Brutus (still looking worried) has stopped, they all descend on the dying man and cut him to pieces to louder

A Crippling Mistake

In this excerpt from his autobiography, Charlton Heston, who played Antony to Jason Robards's Brutus in the film, reminisces about the casting procedure and rehearsals. Heston's appraisal of the Robards's Brutus is sympathetic but brutally frank.

Peter [Snell, the film's producer] had also gotten Sir John Gielgud on board as Caesar. John had played all the other major roles in the play already, as well as those in most of the other plays in the canon; he must've found the casting irresistible. We also had Richard Johnson as Cassius, Richard Chamberlain as Octavius, and Diana Rigg as Portia.

I would play Mark Antony, as I had before. It's the shortest of the great parts, and the easiest—every scene is gold. If you can't play Antony in this play, don't do Shakespeare.

We still had to cast Brutus, the central role in the play. The part has been described as a rough sketch for Hamlet, though not as interesting a role. Jason Robards is among America's best actors. I'd seen him give a superb performance as the elder son in Eugene O'Neill's last and greatest play, *Long Day's Journey into Night,* a season or so before in support of Fredric March. O'Neill is our greatest playwright, but his roles are not actor-friendly. If you can play O'Neill, you can play anything. Or so I thought.

Casting Jason as Brutus turned out to be a crippling mistake. Let me be clear; Jason Robards is a very fine actor. Nevertheless, I still must say that I have never seen a good actor so bad in a good part as Jason was as Brutus. It's true that our director, Stuart Burge, had more experience on stage than in film, and it's also true that Jason was going through a bad time in his life. His marriage to Lauren Bacall was coming to an end; he had other problems as well. Also, Brutus is a knotty kind of role, in which no actor has ever really triumphed . . . but a good actor must be at least good in it. You have to *be* there, make the scenes *work.* Jason was . . . terrible is the only word.

We began with a week of rehearsals in London. Rehearsals in film are not common, nor often useful. Most film people are not really comfortable rehearsing a whole script in advance of the shoot. Still, for Shakespeare, I think it's essential, just to get the actors in form, and remind them of who they're dealing with. The Old Gentleman of Stratford is an awesome partner; you have to take care he doesn't leave you bleeding in the dust.

Charlton Heston, *Into the Arena: An Autobiography.* New York: Simon and Schuster, 1995, pp. 418–19.

chords of music. It is a holocaust, and the rest of the Senate huddle together terrified at the spectacle. An overhead shot shows the conspirators encircling the body, bathing their hands ritually in Caesar's blood.

There are several imaginative touches in the film—Antony's spoken thoughts ('If then thy spirit look upon us now,/Shall it not grieve thee dearer than thy death,/To see thy Antony making his peace—') as he shakes the blood-stained hands of the assassins. Calpurnia's dream with Caesar's statue running blood, and the warnings of the poet Artemidorus incorporated in it, and the fact that the conspirators appear before the crowds in the Forum after the assassination with Caesar's blood still red on their hands. The Forum scene, therefore, Caesar's 'funeral', takes place almost within minutes of the killing—wrong, no doubt, in terms of chronology, but most effective dramatically, and exactly as Shakespeare's text has it. There is much to be said in favour of many aspects of this film, in spite of the stresses and strains of its economies, which show here and there. But it lacks its real heart—the greatness of Brutus, the idealist unable to prevail in a world governed by opportunism.

CHAPTER 3

Other Important Characters in *Julius Caesar*

READINGS ON
JULIUS CAESAR

Caesar: Mightier in Death Than in Life

Henry Norman Hudson

> Many scholars have pointed out that, although Julius
> Caesar's character appears in only a few scenes in
> the play, his presence hovers over all the other
> scenes and events. That presence, the late Shake-
> spearean scholar Henry Norman Hudson suggests in
> this beautifully worded essay, is powerful and often
> menacing because Caesar's stature as a general and
> statesman was so great. In this view, Shakespeare
> did not focus the play directly on Caesar and portray
> him in his prime of power and magnificence be-
> cause to do so would have completely overshadowed
> all the other characters. Rather, says Hudson, the
> playwright wisely chose to show Caesar as he ap-
> peared to the conspirators. The reader or spectator,
> therefore, sees the dictator through their eyes, more
> as an image than a man, "making us share some-
> what in their delusion." The delusion, of course, is
> their belief that they can easily eliminate Caesar and
> restore the Republic. But even in death the great
> man's spirit lives on; and his mighty presence inex-
> orably haunts them and shatters their dreams.

The characterization of this drama in some of the parts is not
a little perplexing. Hardly one of the speeches put into Caesar's
mouth can be regarded as historically characteristic; taken all
together, they seem little short of a caricature. As here represented, Caesar appears little better than a braggart; and when
he speaks, it is in the style of a glorious vapourer, full of lofty
airs and mock thunder. Nothing could be further from the
truth of the man, whose character, even in his faults, was as
compact and solid as adamant, and at the same time as limber
and ductile [flexible] as the finest gold. Certain critics have
seized and worked upon this, as proving Shakespeare's lack of

Reprinted from the Introduction, by Henry Norman Hudson, to *Julius Caesar*, by
William Shakespeare, edited by Ebenezer Charlton Black (Boston: Ginn, 1908).

classical knowledge, or carelessness in the use of his authorities. It proves neither the one nor the other.

DID SHAKESPEARE UNDERSTAND CAESAR?

It is true, Caesar's ambition was gigantic, but none too much so for the mind it dwelt in; for his character in all its features was gigantic. And no man ever framed his ambition more in sympathy with the great forces of nature, or built it upon a deeper foundation of political wisdom and insight. Now this "last infirmity of noble minds" is the only part of him that the play really sets before us; and even this we do not see as it was, because it is here severed from the constitutional peerage of his gifts and virtues; all those transcendent qualities which placed him at the summit of Roman intellect and manhood being either withheld from the scene or thrown so far into the background that the proper effect of them is lost.

Yet we have ample proof that Shakespeare understood Caesar thoroughly, and that he regarded him as "the noblest man that ever lived in the tide of times." For example, in *Hamlet,* he makes Horatio, who is one of his calmest and most right-thinking characters, speak of him as "the mightiest Julius." In *Antony and Cleopatra,* again, the heroine is made to describe him as "broad-fronted Caesar"; and in *King Richard the Third,* the young Prince utters these lines:

> That Julius Caesar was a famous man:
> With what his valour did enrich his wit,
> His wit set down to make his valour live:
> Death makes no conquest of this conqueror.

In fact, we need not go beyond Shakespeare to gather that Julius Caesar's was the deepest, the most versatile, and the most multitudinous head that ever figured in the political affairs of mankind.

HIS SPIRIT AN AVENGING ANGEL

Indeed, it is clear from this play itself that Shakespeare did not proceed at all from ignorance or misconception of the man. For it is remarkable that, though Caesar delivers himself so out of character, yet others, both foes and friends, deliver him much nearer the truth; so that, while we see almost nothing of him directly, we nevertheless get, upon the whole, a just reflection of him. Especially in the marvelous speeches of Antony and in the later events of the drama, both his inward greatness and his right of mastership over the

Roman world are fully vindicated. For in the play as in the history, Caesar's blood hastens and cements the empire which the conspirators thought to prevent. They soon find that in the popular sympathies, and even in their own dumb remorses, he has "left behind powers that will work for him." He proves, indeed, far mightier in death than in life; as if his spirit were become at once the guardian angel of his cause and an avenging angel to his foes.

And so it was in fact. Nothing did so much to set the people in love with royalty, both name and thing, as the reflection that their beloved Caesar, the greatest of their national heroes, the crown and consummation of Roman genius and character, had been murdered for aspiring to it. Thus their hereditary aversion to kingship was all subdued by the remembrance of how and why their Caesar fell; and they who, before, would have plucked out his heart rather than he should wear a crown, would now have plucked out their own, to set a crown upon his head. Such is the natural result, when the intensities of admiration and compassion meet together in the human breast.

SHARING IN THE CONSPIRATORS' DELUSION

From all which it may well be thought that Caesar was too great for the hero of a drama, since his greatness, if brought forward in full measure, would leave no room for anything else, at least would preclude any proper dramatic balance and equipoise [counter-balance]. It was only as a sort of underlying potency, or a force withdrawn into the background, that his presence was compatible with that harmony and reciprocity of several characters which a well-ordered drama requires. At all events, it is pretty clear that, where he was, such figures as Brutus and Cassius could never be very considerable, save as his assassins. They would not have been heard of in after times, if they had not "struck the foremost man of all this world"; in other words, the great sun of Rome had to be shorn of his beams, else so ineffectual a fire as Brutus could nowise catch the eye.

Be this as it may, there is no doubt that Shakespeare knew the whole height and compass of Caesar's vast and varied capacity. It may be regretted that he did not render him as he evidently saw him, inasmuch as he alone, perhaps, of all the men who ever wrote could have given an adequate expression of that colossal man.

It is possible that the policy of the drama may have been to represent Caesar not as he was indeed, but as he must have appeared to the conspirators; to make us see him as they saw him, in order that they too might have fair and equal judgment at our hands. For Caesar was literally too great to be seen by them, save as children often see bugbears by moonlight, when their inexperienced eyes are mocked with air. And Shakespeare may well have judged that the best way to set us right towards them was by identifying us more or less with them in mental position, and making us share somewhat in their delusion. For there is scarce anything wherein we are so apt to err as in reference to the characters of men, when time has settled and cleared up the questions in which they lost their way: we blame them for not having seen as we see; while in truth the things that are so bathed in light to us were full of darkness to them, and we should have understood them better, had we been in the dark along with them.

THE IRONY OF FATE

Caesar, indeed, was not bewildered by the political questions of his time; but all the rest were, and therefore he seemed so to them; and while their own heads were swimming they naturally ascribed his seeming bewilderment to a dangerous intoxication. As for his marvelous career of success, they attributed this mainly to his good luck, such being the common refuge of inferior minds when they would escape the sense of their inferiority. Hence, as generally happens with the highest order of men, his greatness had to wait the approval of later events. He indeed, far beyond any other man of his age, "looked into the seeds of time"; but this was not, and could not be known, till time had developed those seeds into their fruits. Why then may not Shakespeare's idea have been so to order things that the full strength of the man should not appear in the play, as it did not in fact, till after his fall? This view will both explain and justify the strange disguise—a sort of falsetto greatness—under which Caesar exhibits himself.

Now the seeming contradiction between Caesar as known and Caesar as rendered by Shakespeare is what, more than anything else, perplexes. But a very refined, subtle, and peculiar irony pervades this, more than any other of Shakespeare's plays; not intended as such, indeed, by the speakers, but a sort of historic irony,—the irony of Providence, so to

speak, or, if you please, of Fate; much the same as is implied
in the proverb, "A haughty spirit goeth before a fall." This
irony crops out in many places. Thus we have Caesar most
blown with arrogance and goading it in the loftiest style
when the daggers of the assassins are on the very point of
leaping at him. So too, all along, we find Brutus most confident in those very things where he is most at fault, or acting
like a man "most ignorant of what he's most assured"; as
when he says that "Antony can do no more than Caesar's
arm when Caesar's head is off." This, to be sure, is not
meant ironically by him, but it is turned into irony by the
fact that Antony soon tears the cause of the conspirators all
to pieces with his tongue. But, indeed, this sort of honest
guile runs all through the piece as a perfusive and permeat-
ing efficacy. A still better instance of it occurs just after the
murder, when the chiefs of the conspiracy are exulting in
the transcendent virtue and beneficence of their deed, and
in its future stage celebrity; and Cassius says,—

So often shall the knot of us be call'd
The men that gave their country liberty.

and again, a little later, when Brutus says of Antony, "I know
that we shall have him well to friend." Not indeed that the
men themselves thought any irony in those speeches: it was
natural, no doubt, that they should utter such things in all
seriousness; but what they say is interpreted into irony by
the subsequent events. And when such a shallow idealist as
Brutus is made to overtop and outshine the greatest practical genius the world ever saw, what is it but a refined and
subtle irony at work on a much larger scale, and diffusing
itself, secretly, it may be, but not the less vitally, into the tex-
ture? It was not the frog that thought irony, when he tried to
make himself as big as the ox; but there was a pretty decided
spice of irony in the mind that conceived the fable.

CAESAR TRIUMPHS

It is to be noted further that Brutus uniformly speaks of Caesar with respect, almost indeed with admiration. It is his
ambition, not his greatness, that Brutus resents; the thought
that his own consequence is impaired by Caesar's elevation
having no influence with him. With Cassius, on the contrary, impatience of his superiority is the ruling motive: he
is all the while thinking of the disparagement he suffers by
Caesar's exaltation.

> This man
> Is now become a god, and Cassius is
> A wretched creature, and must bend his body
> If Caesar carelessly but nod on him.

> Why, man, he doth bestride the narrow world
> Like a Colossus, and we petty men
> Walk under his huge legs.

Thus he overflows with mocking comparisons, and finds his pastime in flouting at Caesar as having managed by a sham heroism to hoodwink the world.

And yet Shakespeare makes Caesar characterize himself very much as Cassius, in his splenetic [spiteful] temper, describes him. Caesar gods it in his talk, as if on purpose to approve the style in which Cassius mockingly gods him. This, taken by itself, would look as if the dramatist sided with Cassius; yet one can hardly help feeling that he sympathized rather in Antony's great oration. And the sequel, as we have seen, justifies Antony's opinion of Caesar. The subsequent course of things has the effect of inverting the mockery of Cassius against himself.

The final issue of the conspiracy, as represented by Shakespeare, is a pretty conclusive argument of the blunder, not to say the crime, of its authors. Caesar, dead, tears them and their cause all to pieces. In effect, they did but stab him into a mightier life; so that Brutus might well say, as indeed he does at last,—

> O Julius Caesar, thou art mighty yet!
> Thy spirit walks abroad, and turns our swords
> In our own proper entrails.

The Nemesis which asserts itself so sternly in the latter part of the play may be regarded as a reflex of irony on some of the earlier scenes. This view infers the disguise of Caesar to be an instance of the profound guile with which Shakespeare sometimes plays upon his characters, humoring their bent, and then leaving them to the discipline of events.

Cassius the Egotist Versus Antony the Opportunist

Harley Granville-Barker

Harley Granville-Barker (1877–1946) was a world-renowned stage actor, theatrical producer, and literary critic, as well as a respected Shakespearean scholar. In this excerpt from the second volume of his famous *Prefaces to Shakespeare*, he offers masterful analyses of the characters of Cassius and Antony as Shakespeare developed them in *Julius Caesar*. Unlike Brutus, who is an idealist and the "spiritual hero" of the play, says Granville-Barker, Cassius is a cynic and egotist. While Brutus is motivated mainly by concerns for the good of Rome and its people, Cassius is wound up with his own personal hatreds and relentlessly pushes to even the score against the man he most distrusts and dislikes—Caesar. Thin-skinned and demanding of his friends, Cassius can be a cold individual, although Granville-Barker maintains that he reveals a more sympathetic, human side in the later stages of the play.

In contrast to Brutus's idealism and Cassius's self-centeredness, Granville-Barker writes, is Antony's sly, practical, and opportunistic nature. Unlike the pushy, driven Cassius, Antony remains mainly in the background, waiting for the most effective moment to assert himself. Then, in his great speech to the mob, he shows that he is a consummate demagogue, a leader who uses popular prejudices and false claims to gain power. This is why Cassius fears Antony and urges the conspirators to kill him along with Caesar. Cassius's cynicism is a useful tool that might benefit the conspirators. That tool is blunted, however, when Brutus demands that Antony be spared, thereby setting in motion the chain of events leading to the conspirators' downfall.

Excerpted from *Prefaces to Shakespeare*, vol. 2: *King Lear, Cymbeline, Julius Caesar*, by Harley Granville-Barker (Princeton, NJ: University Press, 1963). Copyright © 1963 by the Trustees of the Author. Reprinted by permission of The Society of Authors as Literary Representative of the Estate of Harley Granville-Barker.

Cassius, the man of passion, is set in strong contrast to Brutus, the philosopher; and to stress the first impression he himself will make on us, we have Caesar's own grimly humorous assessment of him:

> Yond Cassius has a lean and hungry look;
> He thinks too much: such men are dangerous. . . .
>   I fear him not;
> Yet if my name were liable to fear,
> I do not know the man I should avoid
> So soon as that spare Cassius. He reads much;
> He is a great observer, and he looks
> Quite through the deeds of men; he loves no plays,
> As thou dost, Antony; he hears no music;
> Seldom he smiles, and smiles in such a sort
> As if he mocked himself, and scorned his spirit
> That could be moved to smile at any thing.
> Such men as he be never at heart's ease
> Whiles they behold a greater than themselves,
> And therefore are they very dangerous. . . .

—a Puritan, that is to say, something of an ascetic [austere recluse], and with the makings of a fanatic in him too. Already it will not be, to Shakespeare's audience, a wholly unfamiliar figure. A dangerous man, doubtless; and as much so sometimes to his friends, they will feel, as to his enemies.

> Into what dangers would you lead me, Cassius,
> That you would have me seek into myself
> For that which is not in me?

the besought Brutus protests. At the best a man difficult to deal with; jealous and thin-skinned; demanding much of his friends, and quick to resent even a fancied slight. His very first approach to Brutus:

> I do observe you now of late:
> I have not from your eyes that gentleness
> And show of love as I was wont to have. . . .

And in their later quarrel the burden of his grievance is

> You love me not.

EGOTISTICAL BUT LOVABLE

An egoist certainly; yet not ignobly so, seeking only his own advantage. Convinced in a cause—as we find him convinced; that Caesar's rule in Rome must be free Rome's perdition—he will fling himself into it and make no further question, argue its incidental rights and wrongs no more, as Brutus may to weariness. For argument will have now become a kind of treason. There lie doubt and the divided mind, which he detests in others, and would dread in himself, since there lies weakness too, while passion will carry him through, and give him power to goad others on besides. Egoist he is, yet not intellectually arrogant. He sees in Brutus the nobler nature and a finer mind, and yields to his judgment even when he strongly feels that it is leading them astray. These principles! It would have been practical good sense to add Antony's death to Caesar's; it was foolish to a degree—rapidly it proved so—to let him speak in the market place later; that was a petty business, after all, about Lucius Pella and his bribes; and to what does Brutus' insistence on his strategy lead them but to Philippi [the site of their ultimate defeat]? It is as if he felt that in some such yielding fashion he must atone for those outbursts of rage that he will not control. And yet, despite exasperating failings, the man is lovable, as those which are spendthrift of themselves can be, and as—for all his virtues—Brutus is not.

Cassius is by no means all of a piece, and makes the more lifelike a character for that. He ruthlessly demands Antony's death (the cause demands it), but in a desperate crisis, with danger threatening, he can take sudden thought for Publius' age and weakness. He has marked respect for Brutus; but he does not scruple to play tricks on him, with the letter laid in the Praetor's chair, the placard pinned to the statue. And, despite his outbursts of passion, he can calculate at times pretty coolly. Why does he not go with the rest on that fatal morning to conduct Caesar to the Senate House? He has said he will go—

Nay, we will all of us be there to fetch him.

—and it will not be sudden timidity, certainly, that sways him. Do second thoughts suggest that since Caesar, as he knows, mistrusts him, his presence may rouse suspicion? Shakespeare leaves this to be implied—or not, since we may not remark his absence. Yet he has been so prominent a figure in the earlier scenes, that we can hardly help remarking it.

Cynicism and Coldness of Passion

He is cynical, and can be brutally downright. While Brutus is appealing to Antony's higher nature (Caesar dead there between them) he comes out plump with a

Your voice shall be as strong as any man's
In the disposing of new dignities.

But his deep affection for Brutus rings true; even in the midst of their quarrel, when he hears of Portia's death, as they mutually say farewell.

BRUTUS. For ever, and for ever, farewell, Cassius!
                   If we do meet again, why, we shall smile;
                   If not, why then this parting was well made.
CASSIUS. For ever, and for ever, farewell, Brutus!
                   If we do meet again, we'll smile indeed;
                   If not, 'tis true this parting was well made.

—there is harmony in the echoing exchange itself; and they do not meet again.

The cynical Cassius shows in the soliloquy:

Well, Brutus, thou art noble; yet, I see,
Thy honourable metal may be wrought
From that it is disposed: therefore 'tis meet
That noble minds keep ever with their likes;
For who so firm that cannot be seduced? . . .

—it is at this very moment that he is scheming to seduce his much-admired friend by the papers thrown in at his window and other such devices. Beneath his enthusiasms and rash humors there is a certain coldness of passion, which gives him tenacity, lets him consider and plan, the tension of his temper never slackening; and it is in this combination of opposites that the man is most dangerous. He will put his very faults to use, do things for his cause that he never would for himself, yet not, as with Brutus, studiously justifying them. His hatred for Caesar the tyrant may well be rooted in jealousy of Caesar the man; if so, he is at no pains to disguise it. But he is incapable of protesting his love for him at one moment, while—on principle—he will strike him down the next.

HIS PRIDE LITTLE MORE THAN A MASK

So forthcoming a man, so self-revealing as he naturally is, what character could better animate the play's opening, and get the action under way? But there must soon come a check. No play can continue at such a strain, to the fatiguing of actors and audience both. It comes with this very soliloquy,

Well, Brutus, thou art noble. . . .

and here, if Shakespeare meant to dig deeper into Cassius' nature, would be the chance. But he avoids it. Brutus is to be the introspective character, the play's spiritual hero, so to speak; and there will not be room for two. Nor (as we said) is Cassius the man to spend time in self-searching, though he urges Brutus to.

So the soliloquy—the only one allotted him—matched against the extraordinary vitality of the earlier dialogue, falls a little flat, runs somewhat mechanically, rather too closely resembles one of those conventional plot-forwarding discourses to the audience, to which Shakespeare has long learned to give richer use; and it demands the final whip-up of that rhymed couplet. At this juncture, then, and for a while longer we learn little more about Cassius. In the scene of the storm that follows he is eloquent and passionate still. But it is the same gamut that he runs. And in the scenes which follow this he strikes the same notes, of a rather arid desperation. Not until the later quarrel with Brutus is he fully and strikingly reanimated; but then indeed the intimacy opens up, of which we shall have felt deprived before. We have no deliberate and explanatory self-confession (that, again, belongs to Brutus), simply an illustrative picture of Cassius in word and action, companion to that earlier one.

He has not changed, yet circumstances have changed him. In that paradox lies the tragedy of such natures. He was jealous of Caesar then, and he has turned jealous of Brutus now; of his friend as he was of his enemy. So Caesar read him aright:

> Such men as he be never at heart's ease
> Whiles they behold a greater than themselves. . . .

He slights Brutus' generalship as he once condemned Caesar's courage. He is as quick and as shrewd and as shrewish as ever. But then it was:

> Well, honour is the subject of my story. . . .

and now he is prudently excusing a rogue, with his own honor in question. The one-time eloquent candor has turned to blustering and scolding. Yet, even while he rages, he knows he is in the wrong. His pride is little more than a mask. And the lofty Brutus has but to soften towards him— one touch of simple humanity suffices—and he breaks down like a child. He is pleading now:

> O, Brutus!
>   What's the matter?
> Have you not love enough to bear with me,
> When that rash humour which my mother gave me
> Makes me forgetful?

And from now on, as if—so we noted—in atonement, he will follow the younger man's mistaken lead, convinced as he is that it is mistaken. He only craves affection:

> O, my dear brother,
> This was an ill beginning of the night:
> Never come such division 'tween our souls!
> Let it not, Brutus.

abases himself—he, the elder soldier—with that

> Good night, my lord.

the now indulgent Brutus quickly preventing him with a

> Good night, good brother.

"OLD CASSIUS STILL!"

But thus it is with these catastrophic natures. They spend themselves freely, but demand half the world in exchange. They behave intolerably, try their friends' patience beyond all bounds, confidently expecting, for the sake of their love for them, to be forgiven. They know and confess to their faults, but with no intention of amendment; you must take them, they say, "as they are."

> Old Cassius still

mocks Antony, when the two meet again, parleying before the battle. And certainly the sharp tongue is by then as sharp as ever. At which point we remark too that the quarrel with Brutus and the reconciliation after have proved to Cassius both relief and comfort. For despite ill-omens, and his unchanged distrust in Brutus' soldiership, he proclaims himself

> fresh of spirit and resolved
> To meet all perils very constantly.

But, the battle joined, in the fury of fancied defeat he will kill his own standard-bearer, and himself, in his impatient despair. Old Cassius still!

ANTONY A DARK HORSE?

> There is a tide in the affairs of men,
> Which, taken at the flood, leads on to fortune. . . .

Mark Antony cannot always talk so wisely, but he takes the tide that Brutus loses. He is a born opportunist, and we see him best in the light of his great opportunity. He stands contrasted with both Cassius and Brutus, with the man whom his fellows respect the more for his aloofness, and with such a rasping colleague as Cassius must be. Antony is, above all things, a good sort.

Shakespeare keeps him in ambush throughout the first part of the play. Up to the time when he faces the triumphant conspirators he speaks just thirty-three words. But there have already been no less than seven separate references to him, all significant. And this careful preparation culminates as significantly in the pregnant message he sends by his servant from the house to which it seems he has fled, bewildered by the catastrophe of Caesar's death. Yet, as we listen, it is not the message of a very bewildered man. Antony, so far, is certainly—in what we might fancy would be his own lingo—a dark horse. And, though we may father him on Plutarch, to English eyes there can be no more typically English figure than the sportsman turned statesman, but a sportsman still. Such men range up and down our history. Antony is something besides, however, that we used to flatter ourselves was not quite so English. He can be, when occasion serves, the perfect demagogue. Nor has Shakespeare any illusions as to what the harsher needs of politics may convert your sportsman once he is out to kill. . . .

A DOUBLE GUISE: POLITICIAN AND GRIEVING FRIEND

The servant's entrance with Antony's message, checking the conspirators' triumph, significant in its insignificance, is the turning point of the play. But Shakespeare plucks further advantage from it. It allows him to bring Antony out of ambush completely effective and in double guise; the message foreshadows him as politician, a minute later we see him grieving deeply for his friend's death. There is, of course, nothing incompatible in the two aspects of the man, but the double impression is all-important. He must impress us as uncalculatingly abandoned to his feelings, risking his very life to vent them. For a part of his strength lies in impulse; he can abandon himself to his feelings, as Brutus the philosopher cannot. Moreover, this bold simplicity is his safe-conduct now. Were the conspirators not impressed by it, did it not seem to obliterate his politic side, they might well and wisely take him at his word and finish with him then and there. And at the back of his mind Antony has this registered clearly enough. It must be with something of the sportsman's—and the artist's—happy recklessness that he flings the temptation at them:

> Live a thousand years,
> I shall not find myself so apt to die:
> No place will please me so, no mean of death,
> As here by Caesar, and by you cut off,
> The choice and master spirits of this age.

He means it; but he knows, as he says it, that there is no better way of turning the sword of a so flattered choice and master spirit aside. It is this politic, shadowed aspect of Antony that is to be their undoing; so Shakespeare is concerned to keep it clear at the back of our minds too. Therefore he impresses it on us first by the servant's speech, and Antony himself is free a little later to win us and the conspirators both.

ANTONY PLAYS A GOOD GAME

Not that the politician does not begin to peep pretty soon. He tactfully ignores the cynicism of Cassius,

> Your voice shall be as strong as any man's
> In the disposing of new dignities.

But by Brutus' reiterated protest that Caesar was killed in wise kindness what realist, what ironist—and Antony is both—would not be tempted?

> I doubt not of your wisdom.
> Let each man render me his bloody hand. . . .

And, in bitter irony, he caps their ritual with his own. It is the ritual of friendship, but of such a friendship as the blood of Caesar, murdered by his friends, may best cement. To Brutus the place of honor in the compact; to each red-handed devotee his due; and last, but by no means least, in Antony's love shall be Trebonius who drew him away while the deed was done. And so to the final, most fitting apostrophe:

> Gentlemen all!

Emotion subsided, the politician plays a good game. They shall never be able to say he approved their deed; but he is waiting, please, for those convincing reasons that Caesar was dangerous. He even lets slip a friendly warning to Cassius that the prospect is not quite clear. Then, with yet more disarming frankness, comes the challenging request to Brutus to let him speak in the market place. As he makes it, a well-calculated request! For how can Brutus refuse, how admit a doubt that the Roman people will not approve this hard service done them? Still, that there may be no doubt at all, Brutus will first explain everything to his fellow-citizens himself, lucidly and calmly. When reason has made sure of her sway, the emotional, the "gamesome," Antony may do homage to his friend.

> Be it so;
> I do desire no more.

responds Antony, all docility and humility, all gravity—though if ever a smile could sharpen words, it could give a grim edge to these. So they leave him with dead Caesar.

THE ANTONY THE MOB NEVER SEES

In this contest thus opened between the man of high argument and the instinctive politician, between principle (mistaken or not) and opportunism, we must remember that Antony can be by no means confident of success. He foresees chaos. He knows, if these bemused patriots do not, that it takes more than correct republican doctrines to replace a great man. But as to this Roman mob—this citizenry, save the mark!—whoever knows which way it will turn? The odds are on the whole against him. Still he'll try his luck; Octavius, though, had better keep safely out of the way meanwhile. All his senses are sharpened by emergency. Before ever Octavius' servant can speak he has recognized the fellow and guessed the errand. Shakespeare shows us his mind at its swift work, its purposes shaping.

> Passion, I see, is catching, for mine eyes,
> Seeing those beads of sorrow stand in thine,
> Began to water.

—from which it follows that if the sight of Caesar's body can so move the man and the man's tears so move him, why, his own passion may move his hearers in the market place presently to some purpose! His imagination, once it takes fire, flashes its way along, not by reason's slow process though in reason's terms.

To what he is to move his hearers we know: and it will be worth while ... to analyze the famous speech, that triumph of histrionics. For though the actor of Antony must move us with it also—and he can scarcely fail to—Shakespeare has set him the further, harder and far more important task of showing us an Antony the mob never see, of making him clear to us, moreover, even while we are stirred by his eloquence, of making clear to us just by what it is we are stirred. It would, after all, be pretty poor playwriting and acting which could achieve no more than a plain piece of mob oratory, however gorgeous; a pretty poor compliment to an audience to ask of it no subtler response than the mob's. But to show us, and never for a moment to let slip from our sight, the complete and complex Antony, impulsive and evaluating, warm-hearted and callous, aristocrat, sportsman and demagogue, that will be for the actor an achievement indeed; and the playwright has given him all the material for it.

A MAN WHO DARES TO RISK THE FUTURE

Shakespeare himself knows, no one better, what mere histrionics [theatrical effects] may amount to. He has been accused of showing in a later play (but unjustly, I hold) his too great contempt for the mob; he might then have felt something deeper than contempt for the man who could move the mob by such means; he may even have thought Brutus made the better speech. Antony, to be sure, is more than an actor; for one thing he writes his own part as he goes along. But he gathers the ideas for it as he goes too, with no greater care for their worth than the actor need have so long as they are effective at the moment. He lives abundantly in the present, his response to its call is unerring. He risks the future. How does the great oration end?

> Mischief, thou are afoot;
> Take thou what course thou wilt!

A wicked child, one would say, that has whipped up his fellow children to a riot of folly and violence. That is one side of him. But the moment after he is off, brisk, cool and businesslike, to play the next move in the game with that very cool customer, Octavius.

He has had no tiresome principles to consult or to expound.

> I only speak right on. . . .

he boasts;

> I tell you that which you yourselves do know. . . .

An admirable maxim for popular orators and popular writers too! There is nothing aloof, nothing superior about Antony. He may show a savage contempt for this man or that; he has a sort of liking for men in the mass. He is, in fact, the common man made perfect in his commonness; yet he is perceptive of himself as of his fellows, and, even so, content.

What follows upon his eloquent mourning for Caesar? When the chaos in Rome has subsided he ropes his "merry fortune" into harness. It is not a very pleasant colloquy with which the fourth act opens.

ANTONY.   These many then shall die; their names are pricked.
OCTAVIUS. Your brother too must die; consent you, Lepidus?

LEPIDUS. I do consent.
OCTAVIUS.   Prick him down, Antony.
LEPIDUS. Upon condition Publius shall not live,
             Who is your sister's son, Mark Antony.
ANTONY.   He shall not live; look, with a spot I damn him.

The conspirators have, of course, little right to complain. But four lines later we learn that Lepidus himself, when his two friends have had their use of him, is to fare not much better than his brother—than the brother he has himself just given so callously to death. Can he complain either, then? This is the sort of beneficence the benevolent Brutus has let loose on the world.

But Antony finishes the play in fine form; victorious in battle, politicly magnanimous to a prisoner or two, and ready with a resounding tribute to Brutus, now that he lies dead. Not in quite such fine form, though; for the shadow of that most unsportsmanlike young man Octavius is already moving visibly to his eclipse.

These, then are the three men among whom Shakespeare divides this dramatic realm; the idealist [Brutus], the egoist [Cassius], the opportunist [Antony]. The contrast between them must be kept clear in the acting by all that the actors do and are, for upon its tension the living structure of the play depends. And, it goes without saying, they must be shown to us as fellow-creatures, not as abstractions from a dead past. For so Shakespeare saw them; and, if he missed something of the mind of the Roman, yet these three stand with sufficient truth for the sum of the human forces, which in any age, and in ours as in his, hold the world in dispute.

Was Cicero Too Timid to Be a Good Conspirator?

James A.K. Thomson

Marcus Tullius Cicero is only a minor character in Shakespeare's *Julius Caesar*. This is mainly because Cicero played no role in Caesar's assassination, the event around which the play revolves. Yet, as noted classical scholar James A.K. Thomson states in this fascinating essay, Shakespeare could hardly ignore Cicero. A senator, consul, republican champion, and the greatest lawyer and orator in Rome, he was without a doubt one of the towering figures of the period and indeed of all Roman history. Shakespeare does more than just include Cicero in the cast, Thomson suggests. He also tries, to some degree, to answer the question of why Cicero did not join the conspirators. In so doing, Shakespeare subtly satirizes him, or pokes fun at him in the literary sense, by calling attention to his scholarly attributes. Cicero is seen as a mild-mannered, rather timid fellow, who does not get involved in the conspiracy because he is too wrapped up in his own little world of scholarly pursuits, among them reading and speaking Greek.

The character of Cicero is a . . . problem of *Julius Caesar*.

CASSIUS. Did Cicero say anything?
CASCA. Ay, he spoke Greek.
CASSIUS. To what effect?
CASCA. Nay, an I tell you that, I'll ne'er look you i' th' face again: but those that understood him smiled at one another and shook their heads; but for mine own part, it was Greek to me.

We have seen how carefully Shakespeare studied his [copy of Plutarch's *Lives*, as translated by Sir Thomas] North for

Excerpted from *Shakespeare and the Classics*, by James A.K. Thomson (London: George Allen & Unwin, 1978). Reprinted with permission of Routledge.

Julius Caesar. It is obvious that he must have read with particular attention all the circumstances of Caesar's assassination, which was the core of the matter for his play. Yet it is
one of these circumstances that Casca, when Caesar turned
upon him after receiving the first wound, cried out 'Brother
help me!' in Greek. Casca then did know Greek, and knew it
so well that in a moment of intense excitement Greek words
came naturally to his lips.

CICERO CERTAINLY SPOKE GREEK

If this were all, we might suppose that Shakespeare, who
was admittedly careless in such matters, had merely forgot-
ten the incident or decided to ignore it. But this will not
cover the case of Cicero. For the circumstance of Cicero's
speaking in Greek is not in Plutarch (or North) at all. It is deliberately invented and inserted in the play by Shakespeare
himself. He must have had a reason for this. Was it only to
raise a laugh? Even if we accept that as an adequate explanation, we have still to ask ourselves why he should wish to
raise a laugh at the expense of Cicero. Of course Shakespeare would not be aware of the fact that to most educated
Romans in Caesar's time Greek was a second language, like
French to Frederick the Great or the Russian aristocracy of
last century. He might perhaps have inferred it from the circumstance that it came natural to Casca and to Caesar, who
spent his last breath in three Greek words ["And you, child?",
given in the play as "Et tu, Brute?"], although this piece of information is not in Plutarch but comes from Suetonius, an
author much read in Shakespeare's time, though possibly
not by Shakespeare. Yet, since he did read North, it is not
likely that he omitted to read North's version of the *Life of Cicero,* seeing that he proposed to make Cicero one of the characters in his play. In that Life he would find ample warrant
for thinking that Cicero was likely to speak Greek. For
Plutarch says that when Cicero came first to Rome 'he was
not greatly esteemed; for they commonly called him the
Graecian and scholar, which are the two words in which the
artificers (and such base mechanical people at Rome) have
ever ready at their tongues' end'.

'Grecian and scholar.' Shakespeare had heard these words
before, though never applied to himself but to Cicero, yes; to
him they applied exactly. If the representation of Cicero in
Julius Caesar appears somewhat unusual, even odd, to us, it

cannot be the result of ignorance on the part of Shakespeare, who had been hearing about him all his life. For Cicero was, with Ovid, the idol of Renaissance scholars. He was their master and model in the composition of what they regarded as artistic prose. There were historical reasons for this into which we need not go. One perhaps should be mentioned. Cicero had been recommended as the unapproachable master of prose style by [the Roman orator] Quintilian, whose authority with the schoolmasters was final. Whatever Latin Shakespeare read at school, it is not unlikely that part of it was some portion of Cicero. It is not likely to have been one of the speeches (which were rather too political for schoolboys), but might have been some of the *Letters* or a book of the *De Officiis* or the *De Amicitia* or the *De Senectute.* At any rate he could not have avoided hearing a great deal about Tully [one of Cicero's nicknames, short for Tullius, his middle name]. Perhaps he heard too much.

THE NERVES OF AN ORATOR AND ARTIST

It is not that the delineation of Cicero in *Julius Caesar* is malicious. But it is slightly satirical. And this must be intentional, because (apart from the jibe about his Greek) the record has been altered. For example, when the conspirators decide not to make Cicero privy to their plot, the only reason given is that

> he will never follow anything
> That other men begin.

But the true reason was quite different, and is clearly stated by Plutarch. It was that the conspirators feared his timidity. So far is Shakespeare's reason from the truth that the usual complaint of historians against Cicero is just that he failed so often to make up his own mind on a policy and then stick to it. He was always looking for somebody to give him a lead, although when the lead was given it is true enough that he did not like to play second fiddle. If he had a consistent policy it was to get the 'governing classes' to agree among themselves. So far was he from disagreeing with everybody. At the same time the charge of 'timidity' needs some explanation. The ancients were no good (or very little) at psychological analysis. They could create character but not dissect it. (It is apt to be the other way with us.) For one thing they had not the requisite terminology. Thus they did not draw much distinction, in words, between physical and moral courage.

CICERO COZIES UP TO OCTAVIAN

In early January, 44 B.C., Cicero, the senator and renowned orator, delivered his Fifth Philippic Against Marcus Antonius, *one of several speeches in which he severely criticized Antony for his warlike moves in the months following Caesar's assassination. In this excerpt, Cicero reveals that he approves of Caesar's violent removal, even though he did not take part in the deed. Cicero also shows that he has woefully underestimated the abilities of Octavian, whom he refers to here as Gaius Caesar (i.e. Gaius Caesar the Younger). This supports the view that by this time the orator was old, with the instincts of a scholar rather than of a politician, and, as Brutus and Cassius must have judged, not "conspirator" material.*

Some people feel envious of Gaius Caesar, and pretend that they are afraid of what he may do. But there is no reason to fear that he will prove unable to exercise self-control, or that our honours will go to his head and he will employ his powers intemperately. Once a man has understood what true glory is, once he feels that the Senate and knights and people of Rome love him and see him as beneficial to our country, then he will realize, senators, that *this* is the glory most worth having.

How I wish that the other Gaius Julius Caesar, his father I mean, had equally endeared himself to the Senate, and to patriotic citizens, in his earliest years! Because he neglected to ac-

They knew, but they could not dissect, the temperament which oscillates between daring and panic. That was the kind of temperament that Cicero had. He showed real courage in facing Catiline [a traitor who tried and failed to topple the government] and in facing Antony—after, it must be said, Brutus and Cassius had run away. But he was not a 'strong' man; he had the nerves of the orator and the artist. At the time of the conspiracy he was old, anxious-minded, shrinking instinctively from deeds of blood and violence. He would have been a very bad conspirator, and the conspirators could see that.

A SCHOLAR OF THE BEST KIND

The most tiresome thing about him was his vanity, and it might be argued—though the context hardly supports the argument—that it was this weakness that Brutus had in his mind when he said that Cicero would not follow anything that other men began. Certainly he was inordinately sensi-

complish this, he squandered his entire brainpower, which was enormous, on the fickle public. And that was how, displaying not the slightest regard for the Senate and loyal Romans, he cleared the way for that enhancement of his power which the free and noble people proved unable to tolerate.

But the way in which his son proceeds is very different indeed. He is liked by everybody, and especially by the people who are most worthwhile. Our hopes of freedom depend on him. As for our own personal safety, he has given this back to us already. We have requested that he receive the highest possible honours; and that is already settled, and they await him. We admire his excellent judgement—there is no need to be afraid that he will do anything foolish. For it *would* be foolish to prefer empty power, envy-provoking wealth, a hazardous, treacherous lust for despotism to authentic, stable, solid glory. Having realized this as a boy, surely he will continue to realize it as he grows older.

But he is hostile, some will object, to certain highly distinguished, reputable fellow-citizens. There is nothing to be afraid of there. Gaius Caesar has shelved his personal enmities and given them up—as a gift to his country. He has made his country his judge; he has entrusted everything he plans and undertakes to the guidance of Rome.

In *Cicero on Government*. Trans. Michael Grant. New York: Penguin Books, 1993, pp. 367–68.

tive to praise and blame, and when touched on the raw would express his feelings in very bitter language. His sarcastic wit was notorious. It is therefore a good touch of Shakespeare's when he makes Brutus say

> Cicero
> Looks with such ferret and such fiery eyes
> As we have seen him in the Capitol,
> Being cross'd in conference by some senator.

But, though this might very well be true of Cicero on a particular occasion, it is not true of the man in general, for by nature he was kindly and placable. So the reader is left with at least a partially false impression of the man as he really was.

The only scene in which Cicero speaks is the third of the first act and even there he does not say much or remain long upon the stage. It is midnight, and there is a violent storm, during which a number of alarming portents occur. Casca and Cicero encounter [each other] in a street. It is not explained why they are out at such an hour—a most unusual time for a Roman or Elizabethan gentleman—especially in such a tempest. But of course Shakespeare's audience would not trouble their heads about that. What has been noted as remarkable is an apparent change in the character of Casca. From being a somewhat cynical humorist, disguising a good deal of penetration under an affectation of rusticity, he has now become a creature of superstitious terrors, speaking rather high-flown verse instead of the colloquial prose he used before. The inconsistency may be only apparent, but there must be some reason for bringing it out; and the choice of Cicero as the foil [contrasting character] that throws it into relief is not at once obvious. It may be said that the rationalizing tone in which Cicero speaks of the prodigies is not unlike the tone he adopts when he is discussing dreams and oracles in the *De Divinatione* [*On Divination*]. But it is most unlikely that Shakespeare is thinking of the *De Divinatione.* I should rather suppose that Shakespeare, knowing that scholars had a tendency to pooh-pooh most of the supposed evidence in favour of the supernatural, attributed that tendency to Cicero. It would then be part of the portrait of him as 'Grecian and scholar'.

In this scene Cicero is treated by Casca with deference and respect. Elsewhere too he is spoken of with respect, as by Metellus:

O, let us have him, for his silver hairs
Will purchase us a good opinion
And buy men's voices to commend our deeds:
It shall be said, his judgement ruled our hands;
Our youths and wildness shall no whit appear,
But all be buried in his gravity.

The picture is of a highly respectable personage, a little rationalistic in his opinions, silver-haired, with fiery, ferret eyes, learned enough to know Greek and to speak it. The portrait is distinct enough to give the impression that some actual scholar may have sat for it. But that is hardly Shakespeare's way. It is much more likely that what we have is a sketch from his hand of a typical scholar of the best kind. Of the best kind, but a scholar; and, since Cicero was that, Shakespeare could not refrain from having a dig at him.

CHAPTER 4

The Unifying Themes of Political Power and Oratory

A Clash of Wills: Politics and Power in *Julius Caesar*

E.A.J. Honigmann

According to this astute and thorough analysis by E.A.J. Honigmann, a former professor of English literature at Britain's University of Birmingham, Shakespeare carefully crafted his presentation of the political themes to fit the social setting of ancient Rome. Honigmann first examines how various of the play's characters use oratory (persuasive speech, rhetoric) to wield or gain power. Then he shows how some exercise or achieve power by imposing their wills on others. It is by the force of his personality, for example, that Cassius wins Brutus over to the conspiracy, and conversely, Brutus's will overpowers Cassius's later, making Brutus the dominant character in the conspiracy. Still, says Honigmann, Shakespeare wisely shows that the supposed "greatness" that the play's politicians gain by their force of will is but an illusion. All are inevitably power-hungry, two-faced, naïve, or otherwise fatally flawed.

All of Shakespeare's history-plays and most of his tragedies deal with political problems, yet his critics, until quite recent times, have refused to take his politics seriously. I am particularly irritated by those who assume that in *Julius Caesar* the political implications are obvious, and are exactly the same as the politics in Shakespeare's other works. The dramatist, we have read often enough, supported the 'Elizabethan settlement', a strong central government that promises the best chance of political order in unsettled times, and would have seen Julius Caesar as a regal figure, the Roman equivalent of Queen Elizabeth. To assassinate Queen Elizabeth would be manifestly wicked, we are told, in the eyes of all right-thinking Englishmen, therefore the murder of Julius Caesar is wicked, therefore all the political and moral questions raised by the play admit of straightforward solutions. Brutus and Cassius should not have done it; Rome needed Caesar, as England needed Elizabeth—is that really what Shakespeare thinks in this penetratingly political play?

Two objections immediately suggest themselves. First, the Caesar-Elizabeth, Rome-England parallels are not as clear-cut as has been suggested. True, the Pope had excommunicated Queen Elizabeth, attempts to assassinate her were frequent in her last thirty years, and rumoured and suspected attempts on her life were even more numerous. The two political parties in *Julius Caesar* loosely reflect the division of Shakespeare's England: Queen Elizabeth suppressed the 'old faith', establishing Tudor Protestantism with herself as head of Church and State, and Caesar threatened the old republicanism, replacing it with a new form of government, which he headed as perpetual dictator. In Rome, as in Elizabeth's England, the old 'order' and the new were indeed locked in battle; Caesar, however, is presented in the play as a dangerous innovator, whereas Elizabeth was hailed as her country's innovating saviour. Caesar and Elizabeth stood for entirely different political values, and so, despite superficial similarities, their political positions are not the same. Even if it was wicked to assassinate Queen Elizabeth, the moral and political implications of a plot against a perpetual dictator are not so easily resolved.

Second: is it likely that someone as brilliantly original as was Shakespeare, in his understanding of individual human beings, would have no new ideas when he analyses groups of human beings, in their political relationships? . . . The moral and political implications of *Julius Caesar* may resemble those of Shakespeare's other plays, yet must be examined separately, and will probably turn out to be unique— as all important features of a Shakespearian play always prove to be unique, the more closely we look at them.

SHAKESPEARE CALLED AN "UPSTART CROW"

When Shakespeare set out to write *Julius Caesar,* in 1599, at the age of thirty-five, a new phase began in his writing-career, whether or not he knew it at the time. Hitherto he had specialised in comedy, and in English history-plays; *Julius Caesar* was not only his first mature tragedy, it was also his first mature play with a consciously non-Christian background: which affects the play's treatment of husbands and wives, masters and servants, suicide, the supernatural—and politics. We can be sure, I think, that the decision to move off in these new directions was not taken lightly. In addition, though, there is another reason for regarding *Julius Caesar* as a very special departure. Shakespeare had been publicly chastised, some years earlier, as an 'upstart crow' who dared to compete with his betters—with the 'university wits', Oxford and Cambridge graduates who flaunted their classical know-how in their plays and poetry. Now, for the first time, Shakespeare himself, though not a graduate, undertook to write a play about classical Rome, aware that any theatre-goer who had been to grammar-school would certainly know about the age of Caesar (the age of Livy, Horace, Virgil), whereas his previous historical plays would not have been subjected to the same expert scrutiny (since English history was not on the curriculum in English schools). So it behoved him to be on his guard: a second public attack on him as an upstart, muscling in on classical territory in which he was not really at home, would have been most unfortunate. Moreover, a new young dramatist had recently appeared on the literary scene, a 'pestilent fellow' with a sharply critical tongue, a bricklayer's son (as his enemies alleged) who had studied the classics more intensively than Shakespeare, and was later to refer to Shakespeare's 'small Latin and less Greek'. Ben Jonson, and others, could be expected to look for faults in Shakespeare's play—and indeed we know that Jonson pounced on *Julius Caesar.* . . .

Writing a play about Julius Caesar therefore involved several kinds of risk. The man from provincial Stratford, who was rumoured to have been in his younger years a schoolmaster in the country (Jonson once remarked contemptuously that a schoolmaster 'sweeps his living from the posteriors of little children')—the 'upstart crow', it would be said, was trying to get above himself. And Shakespeare must have anticipated this reaction. How, then, did he prepare for it and try to outflank it?

A PLAY FULL OF SURPRISES

For those who think they know the story of Julius Caesar the play is full of surprises. First and foremost there is the portrait of Caesar himself, falling apart physically and mentally—

deaf in one ear, superstitious, childishly proud of his shrewd judgement, easy game for flatterers (weaknesses largely invented by Shakespeare). This in itself is a warning to us that the dramatist was not afraid of pedantic fault-finders, such as Jonson, and interprets and rearranges history freely, as in the English history-plays. Shakespeare's Cicero, Cassius, and Antony are also surprising—for example, Antony's subservient, almost servile, relationship with Caesar in the first half of the play.

> CAESAR.   Antonius!
> ANTONY. Caesar, my lord!
> CAESAR. Forget not in your speed, Antonius,
>   To touch Calphurnia; for our elders say
>   The barren, touched in this holy chase,
>   Shake off their sterile curse.
> ANTONY.   I shall remember.
>   When Caesar says 'Do this', it is perform'd.
>
> (I.2.4)

According to Plutarch, Antony had already reached high political office, second only to Caesar; Shakespeare transforms Antony into something close to a lackey. It follows that he was *not* trying to impress classicists by painting historically unimpeachable portraits of the Principal characters.

As many commentators have said, Shakespeare's special effort went into the *language* of *Julius Caesar.* Apart from the poets and prose-writers that I have already mentioned (Livy, Horace, Virgil), the Rome of Julius Caesar bred orators, such as Cicero, trained in the schools—and Shakespeare's unique achievement was that he re-created a world dedicated to speech-making and the arts of persuasion. Deciding to go 'extra-territorial' and to compete with dramatists who could boast a finished classical education, the 'upstart crow' invites his audience to attend to a new rhetoric—loosely based on Latin models in its self-conscious artistry, its sheer professionalism. . . .

SPEECHES THAT SWIM AGAINST THE TIDE

Of course, Shakespeare had written many plays before *Julius Caesar* in which 'speech-making' is important, notably *Henry V.* I am not sure why *Julius Caesar* seems more 'classical' in this respect than its predecessors—partly, no doubt, the feeling is influenced by the high concentration of 'Roman allusions'.

> Wherefore rejoice? What conquest brings he home?
> What tributaries follow him to Rome
> To grace in captive bonds his chariot wheels?

You blocks, you stones, you worse than senseless things!
O you hard hearts, you cruel men of Rome
Knew you not Pompey? . . .

(I.1.33)

These, and the many allusions to Roman landmarks and
customs, help to create the impression that we are listening
to 'Roman' oratory. But the rhetoric of *Julius Caesar* differs
from that of Shakespeare's earlier plays in at least one other
point: again and again the big speeches exhort stage-listen-
ers to abandon their purposes, to change their minds. Compare *Henry V*, the nearest rival to *Julius Caesar* in speech-
making, and you find the very opposite: Henry wants to go
to war, and the Archbishop of Canterbury encourages him;
his men are there to fight, at Harfleur and Agincourt, and
Henry cheers them on; at the end, everyone wants peace,
and Burgundy speaks for all. These orations, like the cho-
rus-speeches, lift the listeners by reinforcing a wish or a
mood already present in them. In *Julius Caesar* the orator
swims against the tide, not with it, quells the mood of his listeners, and changes the course of events. The tribune Marullus subdues the skylarking of the plebeians in Act I scene 1,
till they creep away, 'tongue-tied in their guiltiness'; Cassius
talks to an unwilling Brutus, pushing him in a direction he
had not intended to go; Portia also compels Brutus to do
what he had not wished. These are forensic speeches, moving from point to point with a professional expertise till they
reach an irresistible conclusion, which is followed, as often
as not, by a kind of surrender from the listener.

O ye gods,
Render me worthy of this noble wife!

(II.1.302)

This is Brutus's polite way of saying, as many a husband has
said since, 'O God, what a wife!' (He doesn't *quite* say 'O God,
she's got round me again!') And these speeches all lead up to
Antony's 'Friends, Romans, countrymen', where, again, the
rhetoric totally changes the mood of the listeners and drives
them to actions they had not contemplated.

It is, therefore, the professionalism of its rhetoric that so
sharply distinguishes *Julius Caesar* from earlier histories and
tragedies. The speakers, when they want to persuade, know
exactly how to go about their business, because they belong to
a tradition—a Roman tradition—of oratory. One senses this
professionalism when the speaker plays his ace-card to maxi-

mum effect, as a last resort, as when Portia suddenly reveals her wound, or Antony at last spells out the provisions of Caesar's will—namely, that the whole thing was planned, step by step, by one who anticipated and shaped an inevitable response. . . . These . . . are signals to us that the speaker has not drifted aimlessly but has fulfilled a conscious purpose.

WHEN AN ORATOR IS SPEECHLESS

Having observed the technical proficiency of those who resort to rhetoric in *Julius Caesar,* and how effortlessly men and women in this Roman world, in public and private situations, switch on the arts of persuasion, we must next note that a failure to speak effectively becomes all the more meaningful. Julius Caesar, at home *'in his night-gown',* is not only superstitious and pompous, he is positively garrulous—a tendency already visible when he protests too much that he does not fear Cassius.

> Would he were fatter! But I fear him not.
> Yet *if* my name were liable to fear
> I do not know the man I should avoid
> So soon as that spare Cassius. . . .
> I rather tell thee what is to be fear'd
> Than what I fear: for always I am Caesar.
>
> (I.2.198)

Such uncontrolled, 'give-away' speaking is all the more remarkable set beside the highly wrought rhetoric of this play. Similarly, when the uncouth Casca explains how Caesar was offered a crown, and the scene's verse gives way to stumbling prose, a point is made about the standards one could expect from an educated Roman.

> I can as well be hanged as tell the manner of it: it was mere foolery; I did not mark it. I saw Mark Antony offer him a crown—yet 'twas not a crown neither, 'twas one of these coronets—and, as I told you, he put it by once; but for all that, to my thinking, he would fain have had it. Then he offered it to him again; then he put it by again. . . .
>
> (I.2.234)

He pours it all out, drawing from Brutus the remark

> What a blunt fellow is this grown to be!
> He was quick mettle when he went to school.
>
> (294)

Brutus refers disparagingly to one who does not know how to express himself properly, though he would have been told how in elegant lectures 'when he went to school'.

Even more significant than the gap between careless and careful speakers is the contrast between different kinds of competence exhibited by a single speaker. Brutus's Forum-speech proves him to be highly skilled in oratory. . . . When the conspirators meet at his house, Brutus also speaks fluently. All the more surprising, therefore, that so practised a speaker seems so helpless when Portia sets about him, that he wards off her rhetorical flow with short phrases totally devoid of rhetorical art—

> I am not well in health, and that is all.

(II.1.257)

She persists—

> Brutus is wise, and, were he not in health,
> He would embrace the means to come by it.

He shrugs—

> Why, so I do. Good Portia, go to bed. . . .

I believe that, although his short replies to Portia are sometimes spoken as if he is only half-listening to her (a typical husband?), a more likely explanation is that he is overwhelmed by her vehemence. For a while the skilled orator is speechless.

Brutus's feeblest speech, in my view, comes at the end of the quarrel-scene, when he plucks up courage to address that 'monstrous apparition', the Ghost of Caesar.

> BRUTUS. Speak to me what thou art.
> GHOST. Thy evil spirit, Brutus.
> BRUTUS. Why com'st thou?
> GHOST. To tell thee thou shalt see me at Philippi.
> BRUTUS. Well; then I shall see thee again?
> GHOST. Ay, at Philippi.
> BRUTUS. Why, I will see thee at Philippi then. [*Exit* GHOST.]

(IV.3.279)

This is an extraordinary example of not knowing what to say: 'Why, I will see thee at Philippi then—if you say so.' The fact that in Plutarch almost the same words are used would be no excuse for such a feeble line—except that feebleness is right at this moment, expressing Brutus's shock and confusion, which he admits in the very next line: 'Now I have taken heart thou vanishest.'

In this play, then, we find a complete rhetorical range, from formal orations and other long speeches that set out to persuade down to mumbled excuses and near-helpless echoing of what another has said. Perpetually switching from speech-making to talk, from one register to another, Shakespeare draws attention to rhetoric as a basic fact of Roman life, a mental discipline that he has woven into the fabric of this studiously Roman play, just as he very deliberately threads in allusions to Roman history and topography. . . .

WILL TRIUMPHS OVER REASON

So far I have argued that in *Julius Caesar* Shakespeare presents a Roman world highly conscious of the powers of rhetoric, one where the skilled orator uses words as weapons that can change the course of events. The tribune Marullus and Cassius in Act I; Portia in Act II, and Decius Brutus, persuading Caesar to go to his death; Mark Antony in Act III—these are some of the prize exhibits of what rhetoric can actually achieve. But Shakespeare was not so naïve as to believe that the best argument, or the best speech, always wins, in a political situation. The very opposite is often true. This very 'political' play shows, again and again, that crucial decisions are made because one person imposes his *will* on others; Shakespeare rewrites history to prove that the man who can dominate others by force of personality, rather than force of argument, must rise to the top. The 'man of destiny', the Napoleonic man . . . may employ argument, but wins political battles because he or she is the dominant baboon in a wilderness of monkeys—he is 'constant as the northern star' to the conviction that he is always right, 'for always I am Caesar'. As Napoleon put it, 'Wherever I am not, there is chaos'—expressing the supreme self-confidence that is both the strength and the fatal flaw of every Caesar . . . in history.

Shakespeare underlines this point most unmistakably in dramatising Brutus's ascendancy over his fellow conspirators. In Act II, Cassius makes several proposals and Brutus, every time, immediately makes counter-proposals—and anyone who knows the story knows that Brutus's are errors of judgement. If only Cicero had been brought into the conspiracy, as Cassius wished, Cicero—the greatest orator of his generation—could have presented the case for the murder of Caesar so much more convincingly than Brutus that Antony would not have dared to turn the tide of opinion. If only Antony had been killed with Caesar, or had been forbidden to speak at Caesar's funeral, the course of history might have been different. Shakespeare draws attention to the fact that

something other than reason prevails when Brutus compels
Cassius, against his better judgement, to march to Philippi.

> BRUTUS.   What do you think
> Of marching to Philippi presently?
> CASSIUS. I do not think it good.
> BRUTUS. Your reason?
> CASSIUS.   This it is:
> 'Tis better that the enemy seek us;
> So shall he waste his means, weary his soldiers. . . .
>
> (IV.3.194)

But Brutus, having just won the clash of wills in the quarrel-
scene, loftily insists that he knows best. 'Good reasons must, of
force, give place to better.' Cassius still objects, Brutus remains
arrogantly overbearing, and at last Cassius submits. 'Then, with
your will, go on.' A curious phrase, 'Then, with your will, go on.'
How many times, one wonders, have cabinet ministers . . .
mumbled their submission, against their better judgement, in
similar words? 'Then, with your will, go on, Prime Minister.'

Not only in the clashes of Brutus and Cassius but in many
other scenes Shakespeare is concerned, in *Julius Caesar,*
with the triumph of will over reason. Whatever powers the
aging Julius Caesar of the play has lost—and the commentators are agreed that Shakespeare chose to depict the great
Roman in decline—we are left in no doubt that Caesar believes himself to be pre-eminent because he sees himself as
a man of irresistible will.

> And tell them that I will not come to-day.
> Cannot, is false; and that I dare not, falser;
> I *will* not come to-day. Tell them so, Decius. . . .
> The cause is in my will: I will not come.
>
> (II.2.61)

The play shows, of course, that one's strength of will can decline, as do other mental and physical abilities, but Caesar's
vision of himself as the man of unshakable purpose, even if
grotesquely untrue of the man he has become, reveals what
he was, or believed himself to be, when he rose to the top as
'the noblest man / That ever lived in the tide of times'. You
may outlive yourself, and lose your decisiveness (as
Napoleon did) but you remember what it was that lifted you
above the common pack of men. . . .

STRENGTH OF SPIRIT

Shakespeare shows that a leader of men, whether Caesar or
Brutus, may misunderstand people, arguments, and even

the very situation in which he finds himself, and yet can dominate others, who see more clearly, by sheer force of will. This shocking political insight—so very different from the dear old 'Elizabethan World Picture'—emerges as the 'philosophy of history' in *Julius Caesar*, if I may use so grand a phrase. For the play undeniably suggests that the *next* 'man of destiny', though neither outstanding as a general nor as a thinker, possesses the one gift that matters.

ANTONY. Octavius, lead your battle softly on,
Upon the left hand of the even field.
OCTAVIUS. Upon the right hand I: keep thou the left.
ANTONY. Why do you cross me in this exigent?
OCTAVIUS. I do not cross you; but I will do so.

(V.1.16)

Shakespeare's thesis, that sheer will-power is the decisive political factor and overcomes almost all opposition, surfaces in many ways.

Nor stony tower, nor walls of beaten brass,
Nor airless dungeon, nor strong links of iron,
Can be retentive to the strength of spirit. . . .

(I.3.93)

Brutus's interview with Portia is another example. It begins as quiet pleading, and ends as a fearful clash of wills, when Portia discloses the 'great gash' in her thigh. The fact that she was able to bide her time, while the blood was flowing beneath her robes, until the psychological moment when the sight of her wound will destroy Brutus's resistance, proves *her* 'strength of spirit', *her* will to succeed. Not her eloquence, but this exercise of pure will, overcomes Brutus. . . .

[The renowned Shakespearean scholar] A. C. Bradley once remarked that the quarrel-scene in *Julius Caesar* 'can hardly be defended on strictly dramatic grounds'. Perhaps we can defend it by saying that it presents the play's most exciting clash of wills, bringing to a head one of its central interests, which, we may add, explains Shakespeare's rearrangement of some of the incidents of the Forum-scene. . . .

In Plutarch [the ancient Greek writer whose *Parallel Lives* was the main source for the play], the contents of Caesar's *testament* are published *before* Antony's funeral oration; in Shakespeare, we hear almost invariably of Caesar's *will*, and its contents are revealed later, as the climax of Antony's oration; the plebeians are kept dangling, so to speak, to give maximum repetition to an ominous word that has already caught our attention.

- We'll hear the will. Read it, Mark Antony!
- The will, the will! We will hear Caesar's will! . . .
-   The will! Read the will!
- You will compel me then to read the will? . . .
- Why, friends, you go to do you know not what.
  Wherein hath Caesar thus deserv'd your loves?
  Alas, you know not: I must tell you then.
  You have forgot the will I told you of.
- Most true. The will! Let's stay and hear the will!
                              (III.2.139–40, 155–6, 236–40)

Not only has Shakespeare given greater emphasis to 'the will' by making Antony's oration circle round it, and by verbal repetition. He also contrives to suggest that the man who had dominated Rome by his will ('The cause is in my *will:* I *will* not come') somehow wills the mischief and mutiny that follow from the reading of his testament.

Caesar's *will* survives him as a political force, and, like his 'spirit, ranging for revenge', continues to dominate the Roman world. . . . The *spirit* of Caesar and the *will* of Caesar are just about identical in the play: the Ghost appears as a dismembered, menacing will, and does not even have to explain its reason for coming. Brutus *knows*—

O Julius Caesar, thou art mighty yet!
Thy spirit walks abroad and turns our swords
In our own proper entrails!

                                                    (V.3.94)

A KIND OF POKER GAME

Politics can only be as good as the politicians. Shakespeare seems to have set out to prove that the supposedly great men of Caesar's Rome, despite all their talk about high principles, have been ridiculously overrated—a cynical reappraisal that affects not only Caesar and Brutus but also secondary figures. Cicero, who battled courageously against Caesar's ambitions, becomes an ineffectual bystander in the play. 'Did Cicero say anything?' asks Cassius, after Caesar was offered the crown. 'Ay, he spoke Greek. . . . Those that understood him smiled at one another, and shook their heads'—a glimpse of the man added by Shakespeare that subtly degrades him. Strange, too, that in a play containing such memorable orations, Cicero is given nothing memorable to say.

Shakespeare's cynicism about the heroic figures of the classical past must have astounded his contemporaries, such as Ben Jonson; at times the play reads like a deliberate exercise in debunking. . . . His cool rewriting of history is ev-

ident not only in his portraits of individuals but in many incidental touches—for example, the six lines that begin Act IV
scene 1, where Antony and Octavius and Lepidus haggle
over the lives of a brother and nephew.

> ANTONY. These many, then, shall die; their names are prick'd.
> OCTAVIUS Your brother too must die. Consent you, Lepidus?
> LEPIDUS. I do consent.
> OCTAVIUS   Prick him down, Antony.
> LEPIDUS. Upon condition Publius shall not live,
>   Who is your sister's son, Mark Antony.
> ANTONY. He shall not live; look, with a spot I damn him.

Plutarch thought this proscription quite outrageous. 'In my
opinion,' he wrote, 'there was never a more horrible, unnatural, and crueller [ex]change than this was. For thus
[ex]changing murder for murder, they did as well kill those
whom they did forsake and leave unto others, as those also
which others left unto them to kill.' Shakespeare, however,
made it an even blacker incident by omitting all signs of reluctance, whereas, according to Plutarch, 'they could hardly
agree whom they would put to death: for every one of them
would kill their enemies, and save their kinsmen and
friends'. Shakespeare turns it into a kind of poker-game, a
test of nerves where no one flinches and every man watches
the others for signs of weakness. On the surface, all is harmony and restraint—but, introducing slight pauses, the actors can signal to us that this is not a rational discussion at
all; it is, quite simply, a clash of wills.

The Art and Power of Oratory in *Julius Caesar*

Anne Barton

Julius Caesar is crammed full of examples of oratory and persuasive speeches, both public and private, used to sway both individuals and crowds. In this way, Shakespeare shows that language, when used to its maximum effect, can be a potent means to and function of power. Cassius's ultimately successful attempt to persuade Brutus to join the conspiracy and Antony's manipulation of the mob in the Forum after the assassination are two obvious examples. In this essay, Shakespearean scholar Anne Barton, author of *Shakespeare and the Idea of the Play* (1969), explores these and other examples of the art of persuasion in *Julius Caesar*. Barton contends that persuasive speech also has the power to turn inward on and destroy the speaker. She demonstrates how the characters are sometimes deceived by their own oratory, as when Brutus is actually convinced that he and the other conspirators, having killed Caesar, are "sacrificers," not "butchers"; and later, when Brutus addresses the mob and believes his own excuse about killing Caesar for the good of Rome.

On the eve of Caesar's assassination, when the heavens rain down fire and Rome is filled with prodigies and portents, Casca encounters Cicero in the streets. Breathless and dismayed, Casca pours out a tale of marvels, abnormalities which, he believes, must prefigure some calamity to the state. Cicero, who remains icily calm, admits that

> Indeed, it is a strange-disposed time;
> But men may construe things after their fashion,
> Clean from the purpose of the things themselves.

Excerpted from Anne Barton, "*Julius Caesar* and *Coriolanus*: Shakespeare's Roman World of Words," by Anne Barton, in *Shakespeare's Craft: Eight Lectures*, edited by Philip H. Highfill. Copyright © 1982 by The George Washington University. Reprinted by permission of the publisher, Southern Illinois University Press.

For Elizabethans, this warning of how language may misrepresent fact, how words—whether involuntarily or on purpose—can falsify phenomenal experience, must have seemed especially striking on the lips of Cicero: acknowledged grand master of the art of persuasion, the greatest orator and rhetorician of the ancient world. Shakespeare's Cicero makes no attempt himself to interpret the terrors of the night. He rests content with the neutral observation that disturbed skies such as these are not to walk in, then leaves the stage. In the very next moment, Cassius enters and Casca finds himself confronting a man who proceeds at once to construe things "clean from the purpose of the things themselves" and, what is more, makes Casca believe him. By the end of the scene, Casca has not only accepted Cassius' very different view of the tempest as a reflection of the diseased and monstrous condition of Rome under Caesar's rule, he has agreed as a result to join the conspirators and end that rule through an act of violence. In doing so, he helps to bring about precisely that cataclysm, that condition of anarchy and upheaval that, initially, he feared.

Although Cicero has no part in the action of *Julius Caesar*, it seems to have been important to Shakespeare that the audience should, from time to time, be reminded of his presence and of the controversy associated with his name. In the second scene of act I, Cicero passes across the stage twice as a member of Caesar's entourage. Brutus as bystander remarks on the discontent in his eyes. Casca says that after Antony's abortive effort to crown Caesar, Cicero spoke in Greek and that those who understood him smiled and shook their heads. In act II, after the scene with Casca, Cicero's name is introduced again when Brutus insists upon overruling his confederates and excluding him from the conspiracy on the highly suspect grounds that "he will never follow anything / That other men begin." At Sardis, in act IV, Cassius is shocked to learn that Cicero was one of the senators proscribed by the triumvirs and that he is dead. It is a scattered collection of references but, I believe, purposeful. By keeping the enormous memory of Cicero alive in his tragedy, Shakespeare constantly directs his audience's attention towards Rome as the city of orators and rhetoricians: a place where the art of persuasion was cultivated, for better or for worse, to an extent unparalleled in any other society. . . .

SLICK, PROFESSIONAL ORATORY

[In fact] *Julius Caesar* . . . opens with a scene of persuasion. The Roman citizens in this play, however, are entirely passive: mere puppets manipulated by others. They do not engage in debate . . . neither among themselves nor with the tribune Flavius. The cobbler, the carpenter, and their associates arrive in holiday attire, intending to shout themselves hoarse at great Caesar's triumph. When Flavius has finished speaking to them, they vanish ("tongue-tied," as he says contemptuously) to their homes, obscurely certain without any reasons having been advanced that Caesar is a bad thing, while Pompey was somehow splendid. They will reverse themselves quite as irrationally in act II, with far more serious consequences, when Brutus makes the tactical mistake of permitting Mark Antony to speak last—the position which the historical Cicero always advocated—in Caesar's funeral.

Public oratory in *Julius Caesar* is slick and professional. . . . Flavius, unlike Menenius, has been reading textbooks in the art of rabble-rousing. With its carefully spaced rhetorical questions, deceptive logic, emotive vocabulary, and hypnotic repetitions—"And do you now put on your best attire? / And do you now cull out a holiday? / And do you now strew flowers"—his speech is calculated to drown reason in passion. So, of course, is Antony's even more accomplished appeal to the crowd later on. Nonetheless, although Antony immediately turns the mutiny he has stirred up to his own political advantage—even truncating those legacies to the people of which he had made such capital in describing Caesar's will—he does at least share some of the emotion that he arouses in others on behalf of Caesar dead. "That I did love thee, Caesar, O, 'tis true." Flavius' tears for Pompey, on the other hand, are purely crocodilian. His real reason for tampering with the citizens emerges only after they have slunk guiltily off the stage:

> These growing feathers pluck'd from Caesar's wing
> Will make him fly an ordinary pitch,
> Who else would soar above the view of men
> And keep us all in servile fearfulness.

This is the hidden but real issue, not only of Flavius' speech but of much of the play.

INFLUENCE AND SELF-DELUSION

Almost all the talk about democracy, freedom, tyranny, and restraint in *Julius Caesar* is really a camouflage for something else. Shakespeare's Caesar happens to be deaf in one ear, childless, subject to epileptic fits, vain, superstitious, and as likely to drown in a wintry river or succumb to a fever as soon as any other mortal. Despite these obvious shortcomings, he is also a Colossus: a man over life-size who has created and can control an empire. Cassius says angrily that "this man / Is now become a god," but the real difficulty is that he has not. Gods, after all, are exempt from our envy precisely because they belong to a different order of being. Competition is out of the question, and so is the kind of jealousy that springs from a resented inferiority. Caesar's various human failings are really more exacerbating than his genius, because they remind lesser men, running in the same race with the same handicaps, that they have been far outstripped. Cassius articulates this response most fully, but it is one that many other Roman patricians share, not least— as Cassius knows—the noble Brutus.

In *Julius Caesar,* the art of persuasion has come to permeate life so completely that people find themselves using it not only to influence others but to deceive themselves. This is true, above all, of Brutus. Brutus is competent enough as a public orator, although he lacks the fire and subtlety of Mark Antony, but his real verbal ingenuity declares itself only when he is using the techniques of oratory to blind himself and (occasionally) his friends. In the orchard soliloquy of act II, Brutus extracts purpose and resolve not from the facts of the situation but from a collection of verbal nothings: from words like "may" and "would." There is no tangible basis for Brutus' fears of Caesar. Indeed, as he admits, observation and circumstance suggest the contrary. He is driven, as a result, to do the thing for which he secretly longs—kill Caesar—purely on the basis of a grammatical construction: a verbal emptiness which pretends to have the status of a fact. "Then lest he may, prevent." Antony had said of Caesar earlier in the play that his words were precisely equivalent to deeds: "When Caesar says, 'Do this,' it is performed." Brutus too tries to blur the distinction between speech and action, but the effect he creates is one of self-delusion rather than power.

THE ART OF DEADLY PERSUASION

Shakespeare's Caesar likes to refer to himself in the third person. "Speak, Caesar is turned to hear," he says to the soothsayer in act 1, and in later scenes he resorts to this kind of self-naming almost obsessively. Shakespeare knew, of course, that the historical Caesar had written his commentary on the Gallic Wars in the third person, but there is more behind the mannerism . . . than a mere literary practice. Self-naming implies taking oneself very seriously. It is a deliberately grand way of regarding one's own identity, as though that identity were already matter for historians. Antony is never guilty of it in *Julius Caesar*. He delivers all of his great oration in the first person. Brutus, by contrast, not only employs this peculiarly Roman form of the royal "we" in his defense to the citizens, he uses the third person repeatedly in private conversation. "Brutus," he tells Cassius, "had rather be a villager / Than to repute himself a son of Rome / Under these hard conditions." The effect of these persistent presentations of Brutus by Brutus as a somehow externalized object is to suggest that, although this man is in many ways noble, he is also far too aware of the fact. Indeed, it suggests an underlying affinity with Caesar: the man Brutus kills, supposedly, because Caesar was ambitious.

Cassius plays upon this failing. His persuasion is as deadly as it is because it recognizes and takes advantage of a deeply buried jealousy of Caesar, lurking behind all of Brutus' avowed republican principles, a jealousy which happens to be less conscious than his own. He harps upon Brutus as public figure, the cynosure [center of attention] of every eye, whose ancestors drove the kings from Rome: a man whose scope and potentialities for greatness have somehow been cabined, cribb'd, confin'd by the rival presence of Caesar. He makes Brutus feel that he must commit a spectacular public act in order to validate his name. In doing this, Cassius is less than honest. His victim, however, not only plays into his hands but betters his instruction.

BLOOD STANDS FOR FREEDOM?

In the orchard soliloquy of act II, Brutus turned the techniques of oratory against his own conscience. He continues to do this throughout the remainder of the play. The man who pretends, in act IV, that he does not know about his wife's death, purely in order to impress Messala with the superhuman fortitude of the hero encountering pain, also tries to delude himself that the conspiracy is a kind of holy league. This is why he refuses to countenance an oath to bind its members. Even worse, he uses language dishonestly . . . when he tries to persuade the conspirators that Caesar's death will be not a butchery but a religious sacrifice:

> We all stand up against the spirit of Caesar,
> And in the spirit of men there is no blood.
> O, that we then could come by Caesar's spirit,
> And not dismember Caesar.

They must, he claims, be "called purgers, not murderers." The names make all the difference.

In the event, the spirit of Caesar is precisely the thing they do not kill. They merely release it from the shackles of its human form and failings. No longer deaf, arrogant, epileptic, or subject to error, this spirit walks abroad as a thing against which, now, there is no defense. At Philippi, it turns the swords of the conspirators into their own proper entrails. It raises up a successor in the form of Octavius, who will annihilate the republic in Rome. Even before this happens, Brutus' appeal to the transforming power of words has become half desperate. In the spirit of men there is no blood. But blood, in the first scene of act III, is the element in which the conspirators are drenched. It dyes all of them scarlet, sticks to hands as well as to daggers, disgustingly daubs their faces and their clothes. Not even Brutus can pretend not to notice the sheer physical mess. Characteristically, he tries to spiritualize it, to alter its character by linguistic means:

> Stoop, Romans, stoop,
> And let us bathe our hands in Caesar's blood
> Up to the elbows, and besmear our swords:
> Then walk we forth, even to the market-place,
> And waving our red weapons o'er our heads,
> Let's all cry, "Peace, freedom, and liberty!"

Blood is not blood, he insists, but purely symbolic. It stands for the idea of freedom. The euphemism, and the action with which it is connected, is one of which the second half of the twentieth century has heard all too much.

THE POWER OF LANGUAGE

Brutus ends almost where he began. Rome moves on, and leaves both men behind. The last words of Brutus are not furious . . . but they are . . . hard to accept. "In all my life," he says proudly, "I found no man but he was true to me." In Shakespeare, although not in Plutarch, Messala has already defected to Caesar, as Strato bitterly points out. Nor will time to come necessarily endorse Brutus' last vision of himself: a vision in which, characteristically, he is still presenting himself in the third person.

> I shall have glory by this losing day
> More than Octavius and Mark Antony
> By this vile conquest shall attain unto.
> So fare you well at once; for Brutus' tongue
> Hath almost ended his life's history. . . .

Antony, as one might expect, is generous. "This was the noblest Roman of them all." He leaves us with the image of a Brutus who was gentle, devoid of envy, and perfectly temperate and well balanced: not at all the Brutus who was vulnerable to the persuasions of Cassius, the rash and intemperate man of the quarrel in act IV, who gave the word too early at Philippi. "In your bad strokes, Brutus, you give good words," Antony had said shrewdly before. He forgets these criticisms now. Funeral orations tend, of course, to be false—whether out of good will and compassion for the dead, or because it seems necessary now to tidy everything up in accordance with the demands of piety and decorum. . . . Antony's encomium on the dead Brutus comes nearer truth, but it is far from satisfactory or complete. The meanings inherent in the [story] of Brutus cannot be extracted from funeral orations. They require language of another kind: language that is both further from the facts of the situation and, in another sense, closer.

A Clash of Aims: The Use and Abuse of Oratory by Brutus and Antony

Derek Traversi

The most blatant and powerful examples in *Julius Caesar* of the use of oratory to achieve personal ends are the famous back-to-back speeches delivered by Brutus and Antony in Rome's main square immediately following Caesar's assassination. This thorough and useful analysis of the speeches is from *Shakespeare: The Roman Plays,* a well-respected work by the noted literary scholar, Derek Traversi. Traversi appropriately calls the oratorical dual a "clash of aims" in which each man tries to manipulate the collective will of the mob, always a powerful force in ancient Rome. Brutus's speech, Traversi states, is well-meaning but ultimately shows the character's self-ignorance and foreshadows his own doom. By contrast, Antony successfully plays on the crowd's emotions, demonstrating that the "fickleness of popular emotion" can be a powerful tool in the hands of an effective politician.

The famous oration scene (III. ii) . . . shows a Brutus caught in the consequences of his own act, deprived—now that the mood of exaltation which accompanied him to it has passed—of the impulse to go further, exposed in his inadequate estimate of himself and his situation. Against it is set an Antony who, in the act of appearing as the adventurer and theatrical orator he is, is also the instrument by which the *truth* about murder, which Brutus' idealism cannot cover, emerges to the light of day. This clash of aims and temperaments takes place before a background provided by

Reprinted from *Shakespeare: The Roman Plays,* by Derek Traversi, with the permission of the publishers, Stanford University Press, and the original publisher, The Bodley Head. Copyright © 1963 by Derek Traversi.

a new element in the action: the Roman populace. The crowd has not hitherto played a decisive part in events, though its fickleness has been indicated more than once in the early scenes. It now makes the voice of its appetites heard in a more sinister fashion, thereby showing from still another point of view the nature of the forces which Brutus and Cassius have so irresponsibly released from their normal restraints.

There is, indeed, a sense as though of hunger in the insistent clamour with which the scene opens: 'We will be satisfied: let us be satisfied.' A collective will, primitive and irresponsible, but none the less exacting in its demands, has entered the action. The drama to be enacted over Caesar's corpse will take place in the presence of this force, which could well end by devouring both the contending parties. When the Second Citizen announces his intention of 'comparing' the reasons offered by the speakers, a new if unconscious factor of judgement is asserting itself.

THE SHORT-SIGHTEDNESS OF BRUTUS'S SPEECH

Brutus' oration, as has often been noted, is cold in its balanced abstraction, the utterance of one whose devotion to 'nobility' leads him to the illusion that his 'reasons' need only to be stated clearly and with dignity to command the assent of all right-minded and public-spirited men:

> As Caesar loved me, I weep for him: as he was fortunate, I rejoice at it; as he was valiant, I honour him; but as he was ambitious, I slew him. [III. ii. 26.]

The balanced periods aim, not at emotional appeal, which has no place in the speaker's 'philosophy', but at the statement of propositions demanding assent; and the conclusion—'I slew him'—covers a certain self-sufficiency in its readiness to assume the responsibility for murder. The man who speaks thus is undeniably noble, but his nobility is dangerously close to self-ignorance. 'I have done no more to Caesar than you shall do to Brutus': a note of unconscious irony again asserts itself, together with the incongruous touch of attempted demagogic appeal in the offer of 'a place in the commonwealth' to Mark Antony and his friends: 'as which of you shall not'. Brutus is still unaware of the complexity of his own motives, and this unawareness makes itself felt in the ominous shadow or his conclusion: 'as I slew my best lover for the good of Rome, I have the same dagger for myself, when it shall please my country to need my death.' [III. ii. 49.]

As Brutus brings this speech of self-justification to a close, the crowd begins to play its part. The acclamation of the republican idealist culminates, with a bitter and appropriate irony, in the suggestion that he, the liberator, should be elevated to replace the dictator he has killed. 'Let him be Caesar': the anonymous acclamation is, in effect, a death-blow to all Brutus' idealistic hopes, and it is evidence of the short-sightedness with which he meets it that his last words, urging his hearers to remain with Antony, though in fact an attempt to turn to his own favour the concession offered to his rival, amount to a connivance at his own doom. Strong in the illusion of self-confidence which his nature demands, Brutus leaves the field to an enemy who is particularly equipped to destroy him.

ANTONY CASTS A SHADOW ON HIS ENEMIES

Faced by the initial hostility of the mob, Antony proceeds with caution. He has come, he says, not to 'praise' Caesar, but merely to bury him. As he warms to his task, however, doubt is cast upon Caesar's alleged 'ambition'—

> The noble Brutus
> Hath told you Caesar was ambitious:
> *If it were so,* it was a grievous fault—[III. ii. 83.]

more particularly by comparison with the tangible horror of his end: 'And grievously hath Caesar answer'd it'. As the doubt begins to come home to his audience, Antony feels strong enough to cast a shadow upon the alleged 'honour' of his enemies, to recall the dead man's generosity and to point to his refusal of the crown. By the end of this process the recognition of Brutus as 'honourable' has turned to the implied doubt of 'And *sure,* he is an honourable man'. It may be, indeed, that the certainty is false, though the moment has not yet come to say so openly:

> I speak not to disprove what Brutus spoke,
> But here I am to speak what I do know. [III. ii. 106.]

All his hearers once loved Caesar, 'not without cause': all therefore have a right, even a human duty, to mourn his passing. It is typical that Antony, who—unlike Brutus—appeals consciously to the emotions and finally rouses an element in man not far removed from the bestial, should claim to speak in the name of reason:

> O judgement! thou art fled to brutish beasts,
> And men have lost their reason. [III. ii. 110.]

Having reached the opening point in his campaign to assert his control over his hearers, Antony pauses to allow the effect of his insinuations to sink home.

Each stage in the change of dramatic mood is marked by the comments of his hearers. They first greet him with doubt and resentment—"Twere best he speak no harm of Brutus here'—and to this mood the speaker has been careful to defer. 'For Brutus' sake, I am beholding to you' is the ingratiating preface with which he mounts the rostrum: but gradually, as he feels his way to mastery, he rises to the bolder questioning of 'What cause witholds you then to mourn for him?' and ends with the effective gesture of feeling overcoming the power to speak:

> My heart is in the coffin there with Caesar,
> And I must pause till it come back to me. [III. ii. 112.]

The response is just what the orator intended. There is 'much reason' in what he says; the death of Caesar may open the way for a 'worse' to take his place. The ambition so recently condemned in the murdered man has now become 'certainly' no part of his nature; the eyes of the speaker, moreover, by a most telling piece of sentiment, are seen to be 'red as fire with weeping'.

APPEALING TO THE CROWD'S EMOTIONS

All this implies, beyond insight into the nature of demagogy [oratory in which the speaker sometimes departs from the truth], something perhaps even more important: the assertion of realities which the conspirators have neglected at their peril and which are already gathering to overwhelm them. The change of emotional climate has become such that Antony can now proceed to a new stage in his manoeuvre. This consists in open play upon the fickleness of popular emotion. Caesar's authority of 'yesterday' is contrasted with his solitude in death: none is now 'so poor to do him reverence'. As always with Antony, genuine emotion is mingled with its conscious exploitation in others. The orator, in the act of disclaiming his intention 'to do Brutus wrong and Cassius wrong', proceeds to stir up his hearers 'to mutiny and rage'. Rather than do them wrong, he will 'wrong the dead', 'wrong myself and you'; and the final reference to 'honourable men' comes, now openly ironic, to point his intention. The culminating moment in this part of the speech is an appeal to the interest of the mob in the reference to the will, which however—following the normal tactic of seeming to withdraw what he offers—he says that he does not 'mean to read'. The height of emotional tension at which he aims has, indeed, still to be reached, and Antony procedes to stimulate it by a sensational use of imagery which unites the evocation of wounds and blood with the 'religious' associations to which his audience most readily responds:

> they would go and kiss dead Caesar's wounds
> And dip their napkins in his sacred blood,
> Yea, beg a hair of him for memory. [III. ii. 138.]

The feeling here typifies the play in its combination of violent external colour and inner emotion. The idea of sacred and bloody relics both heightens the value ascribed to the dead Caesar and points to a deliberate manipulation of popular sentiment.

The appeal to emotion produces the desired effect. The crowd demand to hear the will. Antony, still pretending to refuse, hints ever more definitely at its importance—'It is not meet you know how Caesar loved you'—and rouses the very passions he ostensibly condemns. 'It will enflame you, it will make you mad': the words, seemingly designed to restore calm, create the very excess which they deprecate. The determination of the mob makes itself felt in repeated calls for 'the will'; it is the irony of the situation that the people affirm their power to obtain their desire—'You shall read us the will, Caesar's will'—as they are in fact being moulded to Antony's purpose. One more reference to the 'honourable men' whose daggers 'have stabb'd Caesar', and Antony judges that the time is ripe; but, before acceding to read the will, he makes a last show of unwillingness—'You will *compel* me then to read the will'—and prepares for his disclosure by calling upon his hearers to form a ring about the corpse. In full sight of the wounds, and as Antony descends to still closer contact with his audience, the emotional content of the situation will effectively reinforce the appeal so variously made to simple gratitude, base cupidity, and blind ignorance.

MAKING CAESAR'S BODY A RELIGIOUS RELIC

The third long part of the oration is devised to bring the crowd to join in the speaker's own brilliant, colourful flow of

emotion: 'If you have tears, prepare to shed them now.' Once
more, the emphasis is on wounds and on the blood which,
spilt by traitors, flows with an ease which answers to the
emotion now being expressed. Brutus was 'Caesar's angel',
so that the dead man's blood, when it followed the withdrawn dagger, was, as it were,

> rushing out of doors, to be resolved
> If Brutus so unkindly knocked, or no. [III. ii. 184.]

Here and in the following re-creation of Caesar's fall,
Antony's appeal to sentiment, his calculated release in others of the emotions which it is his own nature easily to feel,
reaches its culminating point. He is now able to appeal to the
natural pieties—

> O now you weep, and I perceive you feel
> The dint of pity: these are gracious drops—[III. ii. 198.]

before he makes his last and supremely effective gesture by
turning from 'Caesar's vesture wounded' to the body of the
victim, 'marr'd, as you see, with traitors'.

It is, indeed, now a religious relic that is being displayed
to call for its own intensity of responding feeling. The response comes in broken exclamations, which stand out
against the wonderfully facile flow of what has gone before,
and leads finally to the sinister call for death and revenge:
'Revenge! About! Sack! Burn! Fire! Kill! Slay!' To the last
Antony follows his method of inciting his hearers by disclaiming the very ends he has in mind. He begs them not to
be stirred up to 'such a sudden flow of mutiny'. Caesar's assassins are still 'honourable', though the reasons for their
deed are beyond the understanding of one who is, like those
who hear him, 'a plain blunt man',

> That love my friend: and that they know full well
> That gave me public leave to speak of him. [III. ii. 223.]

It is essential to the irony which prevails at this point that
this, in part, is precisely what Antony is: though it is equally
true that the conscious orator in him, in asserting this 'plain-
ness', is using it for calculated ends. His self-assumed part is
that of one who has

> neither, wit, nor words, nor worth,
> Action, nor utterance, nor the power of speech,
> To stir men's blood, [III. ii. 225.]

one who can 'only speak right on'; and, having said so much,
he returns by contrast to the rhetorical devices which are
the secret of his success:

I tell you that which you yourselves do know;
Show you sweet Caesar's wounds, poor poor dumb mouths,
And bid them speak for me: but were I Brutus,
And Brutus Antony, there were an Antony
Would ruffle up your spirits, and put a tongue
In every wound of Caesar, that should move
The stones of Rome to rise and mutiny. [III. ii. 228.]

It is the familiar mixture for the last time: the disclaimer of the oratorical gifts and graces he is using, the personification of Caesar's wounds, the rousing of his hearers to mutiny through the mention of 'the stones of Rome'.

CHAOS IS LET LOOSE

The effect is immediately gained. The mob, moving off to burn the houses of Brutus and his followers, forget to listen to the terms of the very will which they so passionately demanded to hear; Antony's reminder—'You have forgot the will I told you of'—is one of the most effective strokes of the scene. As they go off, his last comment is a revealing disclaimer of responsibility. 'Now let it work': the orator, resting on his laurels, looks with satisfaction on his achievement, dwells with a certain pleasure on the chaos he has let loose:

Mischief, thou art afoot,
Take thou what course thou wilt. [III. ii. 265.]

The final effect is a revelation of irresponsibility accompanied by sinister pleasure:

Fortune is merry,
And in this mood will give us anything. [III. ii. 271.]

That, later on, she will assume other moods, ultimately less congenial to the speaker, remains to be seen. Meanwhile, the sinister little episode (III. iii) of the destruction of Cinna the poet for a chance coincidence of name, comes effectively to announce the brutality which will from now on so frequently preside over the course of events.

CHAPTER 5

Other Dramatic Themes and Images in *Julius Caesar*

READINGS ON
JULIUS CAESAR

Distorted Self-Views: Role-Playing in *Julius Caesar*

Thomas F. Van Laan

This perceptive analysis of Shakespeare's famous political play is by Thomas F. Van Laan, a veteran of
the Department of English at Rutgers University. Van
Laan examines the recurring motif of discrepant role
playing, that is, the contrast between the way a character sees his or her social and/or historical role and
the way Shakespeare and we, his audience, see that
character's role. Almost all the important characters
in the play see themselves, in a sense, as actors in a
great historical drama, which, of course, they were.
But in addition, says Van Laan, each views himself or herself in a way that we the spectators can see is actually distorted and false. Caesar suffers from this self-deception, for
instance, by constantly projecting an all-powerful, god-like
image. The audience easily sees through this façade and re-
alizes that he is far from perfect. Similarly, Cassius sees himself as a greater man than Caesar, while we see that he is
just as flawed, or perhaps more flawed, than Caesar. And
Brutus views himself always as a deeply honorable man,
even though we see clearly that his betrayal of Caesar is, at
least on some levels, a dishonorable act. All of these characters, then, hold distorted views of their own natures and of
the roles they are playing in the drama of their times. And
Shakespeare's exploration of the contrasts in perception that
result is part of what makes the play great.

> CASSIUS   How many ages hence
> Shall this our lofty scene be acted over
> In states unborn and accents yet unknown!
> BRUTUS How many times shall Caesar bleed in sport,
> That now on Pompey's basis lies along
> No worthier than the dust!

CASSIUS   So oft as that shall be,
So often shall the knot of us be call'd
The men that gave their country liberty.
                          (*Julius Caesar*, III.i. 112–19)

This trio of speeches is surely meant to be highly ironic. *Julius Caesar* is itself one of the dramatizations of the murder of Caesar which Cassius prophesies for 'states unborn and accents yet unknown,' and thus his excited and joyful vision of these future dramatizations suddenly defines Shakespeare's play as a play. The effect is calculated to make the spectators keenly self-conscious about themselves and their responses, to get them to note consciously how much their responses differ from Cassius' prediction about them. Few members of Shakespeare's original audience would have been sufficiently uninformed to regard Cassius and his fellow conspirators as 'men that gave their country liberty,' and those who were this uninformed had only to wait until the end of the play to realize how inaccurate and inappropriate the designation is. Some spectators undoubtedly agreed that the assassination was a 'lofty' act, but it is highly probable that a far greater number would have . . . regarded Cassius' 'lofty scene' more as the 'savage spectacle' later referred to by Brutus. Those spectators who let their responses be determined less by their own attitudes towards the historical events and more by Shakespeare's dramatization of these events would at the very least have felt that the assassination and the people involved in it are far more complicated than Cassius would allow. These speeches by Cassius and Brutus record therefore (and in a role-playing image) an ironic discrepancy between, on the one hand, the characters' assumptions about their activity and, on the other, its true nature—i.e., those views of it held by Shakespeare and by all those spectators who for whatever reason cannot agree with Cassius and Brutus.

ROMAN ACTORS ALL

Cassius' anticipation of future plays dramatizing the conspirators' act is the most striking of the explicit allusions to role-playing in *Julius Caesar*, but there are several such allusions, and all of them evoke the notion of discrepancy. Casca regards Caesar's rejection of the crown Antony offers him on the Lupercal as a piece of fakery, and it prompts him to see the whole occasion in theatrical terms: 'If the tag-rag people did not clap him and hiss him, according as he pleas'd and displeas'd them, as they use to do the players in the theatre, I am no true man' (I.ii.257–60). Brutus uses similar imagery in advising his fellow conspirators to 'look fresh and merrily':

> Let not our looks put on our purposes,
> But bear it as our Roman actors do,
> With untir'd spirits and formal constancy.
>
> (II.i.224–7)

The conspirators' successful carrying-out of this advice on the morning of the assassination provides an explicit nonverbal image of discrepant role-playing, Antony's later use of the conspirators' own technique against them provides another, and a third occurs on the battlefield in Act V when Lucilius poses as Brutus in order to protect him. Shakespeare has, moreover, already established the motif of discrepant role-playing before introducing this explicit development of it. For when the commoners are milling about the streets of Rome at the beginning of the play, what at first seems most to disturb the tribunes Flavius and Marullus is that these commoners are out of costume and failing to observe the decorum proper to their lots (I.i.1–8)—that, in other words, they are misplaying their social roles.

These evocations of role-playing . . . are merely the outer, explicit dimension of a dramatic design that embraces the entire action of the play. Almost every character in *Julius Caesar* becomes a sort of 'Roman actor' through his participation in discrepant role-playing, and most of them practise the specific form of it embodied in Cassius' anticipation of future dramas. Cassius gives the murder of Caesar a more favourable interpretation than Shakespeare or most of his spectators can accept. He glorifies it, and in so doing, he defines himself as better than he is. This element of self-glorification is absent from most of the explicit evocations of role-playing, but the *act* of projecting a representation of the self which is superior to the reality is entirely typical. It is without doubt the most characteristic act of the play.

Shakespeare's version of the actual striking down of Caesar, for example, is as much as anything else a moment of sardonic humour ironically exposing the absurd pretensions of a self-deluded fraud. Caesar cannot be persuaded to change a decision, he assures Brutus and the others, because he is as 'constant as the northern star, / Of whose true-fix'd

and resting quality / There is no fellow in the firmament'
(III.i.60–2). . . . The appeals persist, however, and Caesar
must make himself more emphatically clear: 'Hence! Wilt
thou lift up Olympus?'. There can be no doubt how this im-
perfect human regards himself, despite his age and infirmity, his partial deafness, and his epilepsy. In his own eyes,
as Cassius has perceived, Caesar is not only the most perfect
of men but even more: a god, a true resident of Olympus.
And so, naturally, he speaks and acts accordingly. But although he strives constantly to play the god, he continually
betrays his human frailty. 'Wilt thou lift up Olympus?' he
cries out; and yet he is about to be struck down by the knives
of his assailants, about to perform the most characteristically human (or 'mortal') act possible, that of dying. This final view of Caesar is in perfect keeping with Shakespeare's
entire presentation of him. While Cassius' account of Caesar's
physical deficiencies (I.ii.93–131) is a complex speech that
says perhaps even more about Cassius than about Caesar, it
does explicitly establish the theme of Caesar's incongruous
assumption of godlikeness ('this god did shake'), and each of
Caesar's subsequent appearances keep this incongruity in
the forefront. Shakespeare's Caesar has scarcely any reality
apart from his highly ironic attempt to play a role for which
he is utterly unfitted.

CASSIUS'S ROLE COMES FROM HIS IMAGINATION

Cassius is a more complex and in many ways a more self-
aware character than Caesar, but he also suffers from self-
delusion, as is revealed by his motive for the assassination.
His eventual characterization of himself and the other conspirators as 'men that gave their country liberty' rings oddly
coming from him because he has clearly held, and all but
expressed, a far more personal motive for killing Caesar. 'I
cannot tell what you and other men / Think of this life,' he
says to Brutus, in broaching the subject of doing *something*
about Caesar, 'but, for my single self, / I had as lief not be as
live to be / In awe of such a thing as I myself' (I.ii.93–6).

Cassius at once enlarges the ranks of those equalling Caesar to include Brutus, and in his next speech he removes himself even further from the centre of attention through his sarcastic talk of '*we* petty men,' his assurance, 'The fault, dear
Brutus, is not in our stars, / But in ourselves, that *we* are underlings' (italics added) and, especially, his insistence that the

name *Brutus* is as fair as Caesar's. Nevertheless, Cassius obviously thinks primarily of himself rather than Brutus or some collective 'we.' In his speech on Caesar's infirmities, he measures Caesar and finds him wanting, not in relation to all men but to himself, and, in keeping with the feeling of superiority this gives him, he views Caesar's political success not as a public scandal but as a personal injustice: 'And this man / Is now become a god; and Cassius is / A wretched creature, and must bend his body / If Caesar carelessly but nod on him'. Furthermore, although Cassius needs Brutus and the others to help him correct this injustice, he certainly does not regard them as his equals in worth. He assumes naturally the role of leader in relation to most of them, and although he flatters Brutus in order to ensure his participation, he considers him as nothing more than a useful tool. This, his true view of Brutus, is amply conveyed by his soliloquy concluding I.ii and by his later remark to Casca: 'Three parts of him / Is ours already, and the man entire / Upon the next encounter yields him ours' (I.iii. 154–6).

Cassius sees himself as the true Caesar; he already plays this role in his imagination, and he seeks, through the conspiracy, to set the stage so that he can also play it in reality. His discrepant role-playing is less advanced than Caesar's but quite clearly a valid and central fact of his identity. His career also differs from Caesar's in that its irony is less explicit, less insistent than the irony of the mortal immortal. But the irony of Cassius' career is fully evident. It is writ large in the failure of the conspiracy and Cassius' consequent death. It is also, moreover, implicit in Cassius' actual position in relation to the two figures that most frustrate his hopes. Despite his feeling of injustice, the fact remains that it *is* Caesar, not Cassius, who has achieved such a high state of success. And although Cassius conceives the conspiracy and seduces Brutus into joining it, it is Brutus, not Cassius, who ends up as the actual leader of the conspiracy. Cassius sees himself as the true Caesar, but in reality he always remains (wherever the fault may lie, in the stars or in himself) an 'underling.' One is almost tempted to say, an 'understudy.'

BRUTUS MORE NAIVE THAN HONORABLE?

The role Brutus claims and plays but cannot really fulfil is the one Antony refers to again and again in his funeral oration. Brutus is, or so he believes, an 'honourable man.' He thinks only of 'the general good' (I.ii.85), can be provoked to act against Caesar only to prevent tyranny, wants the conspirators to 'be sacrificers, but not butchers' (II.i.166), and wishes they 'could come by Caesar's spirit,/And not dismember Caesar' (169–70). He and Cassius both use the word 'honour,' but while Cassius is thinking of personal glory, Brutus means moral purity and integrity, that which compels the good man to act uprightly and to do so in a positive way—that is, by actively making sure that things which should be done get done.

One dramatic fact casting a good deal of ironic light upon Brutus' presentation of himself is Cassius' manipulation of him. Brutus' complete ignorance about what Cassius is doing to him (or, for that matter, about the true state of his entire relationship with Cassius) is in itself sufficient to make him look rather naive and thus cast doubt on any favourable self-impression he might project. Cassius, moreover, deliberately heightens the effect by mocking in his soliloquy Brutus' pretensions to nobleness and honour:

> Well, Brutus, thou art noble; yet, I see,
> Thy honourable metal may be wrought
> From that it is dispos'd. Therefore it is meet
> That noble minds keep ever with their likes;
> For who so firm that cannot be seduc'd?
>
> (I.ii.307–11)

But Brutus' own soliloquy in II.i is even more destructive. Here he expresses more clearly than ever his refusal to act in such a consequential and questionable business as the assassination without just, public motives, and yet, at the same time, he resolves to so act while revealing his utter unfamiliarity with any such motives. This man of perfect honour resolves to kill Caesar because Caesar *may* become dangerous to 'the base degrees / By which he did ascend':

> Then, lest he may, prevent. And since the quarrel
> Will bear no colour for the thing he is,
> Fashion it thus—that what he is, augmented,
> Would run to these and these extremities;
> And therefore think him as a serpent's egg,
> Which, hatch'd, would as his kind grow mischievous,
> And kill him in the shell.
>
> (II.i.28–34)

The decision to take such an important step purely on the basis of possibilities and virtually manufactured suppositions ('Fashion it thus') suggests that Antony may well be right when he later implies that 'honour' is merely an empty word for Brutus. Certainly, it is not a word that Brutus gives thought to, in order that it may have concrete meaning, but one he uses as a substitute for thought, apparently believing that since *he* is 'honourable' whatever he fancies doing must also be honourable. Brutus is perfectly capable of deliberately creating a fraudulent impression, as his behaviour to Caesar demonstrates and as the odd double account of Portia's death may also exemplify, but it seems clear that in playing the fraudulent role of the honourable man he deceives himself as well as others. Like Caesar and Cassius, he holds a distorted conception of his own nature. . . .

ANTONY SEES HIMSELF AS CAESAR'S HEIR

Antony's discrepant role-playing occurs during the second half of the play and closely resembles that of Cassius. His soliloquy near the end of III.i, just after the assassination, is entirely concerned with the horrid revenge he vows to wreak against 'these butchers'; and this, it seems, is the only intention the death of Caesar has occasioned for him. In IV.i, however, as he and Octavius and Lepidus make plans for the future, revenge is not once mentioned. The three triumvirs concern themselves with the political power they will hold once they defeat Brutus and Cassius, and they show that they intend to hang on to it. Antony, moreover, indicates that he regards this power primarily as his own personal possession. He contemptuously dismisses Lepidus as 'a slight unmeritable man / Meet to be sent on errands' (IV.i.12–13), he reminds Octavius, 'I have seen more days than you', and, essentially, it is he that makes the primary decisions in the scene. Antony has clearly assumed the leadership of the triumvirate and regards himself, evidently, as Caesar's heir. But just as Cassius is destined to remain an underling, so is Antony. His reign is short. The next time he appears (v.i), Octavius has already assumed control, though Shakespeare also manages to represent the shift in power within the scene:

> ANTONY Octavius, lead your battle softly on,
> Upon the left hand of the even field.
> OCTAVIUS Upon the right hand I: keep thou the left.
> ANTONY Why do you cross me in this exigent?
> OCTAVIUS I do not cross you; but I will do so.
>
> (v.i.16–20)

Four lines later Antony calls Octavius 'Caesar' for the first time in the play, and by the end of the play the only function he still retains seems to be that of saying nice things about the fallen enemy. The final speech belongs to the new Caesar. It deals with practical arrangements for Brutus' funeral, the disposition of the troops now that the battles have ended, and the dividing of the spoils. It is intrinsically a far less interesting speech than the one by Antony just before it, but it prevents any doubt about who finally guides the destiny of Rome.

A Play About History

The three other characters that participate in discrepant role-playing are much less central to the action, but they help substantially in amplifying its primary theme. Casca's coarse, cynical manner, according to Cassius, is a 'tardy form' that he deliberately 'puts on' (I.ii.298). Cassius thinks that this exterior conceals a genuine enthusiasm for any 'bold or noble enterprise', but the fearful, superstitious attitude Casca reveals towards the storm in I.iii suggests that his tough-guy pose may well be intended to conceal something a little less praiseworthy. Portia believes that her identity as daughter of Cato and wife of Brutus renders her worthy enough for Brutus to take her into his confidence, to share with her the secrets of such obvious import which trouble him, but Brutus has not treated her as she deserves, and this makes her 'Brutus' harlot, not his wife' (II.i.287). Since Brutus agrees to share his secrets with her, and her anguish in II.4 indicates that he has done so, Portia actually becomes what she considers herself to be, but Shakespeare gives far more emphasis to her original expression of failure than he does to her ultimate success—it is the first of these motifs that is the fully dramatized one—and Portia is, moreover, the only one participating in the discrepant role-playing who manages to eliminate the discrepancy. Cinna the poet certainly does not. He has as much right as Portia to actually be what he takes himself to be—he really is, after all, Cinna the poet but the wild mob of III.iii nonetheless determines that he shall for all practical purposes possess a different and less desirable identity: if not that of Cinna the conspirator, at least that of Cinna the victim of their vengeance.

The examples of Portia and Cinna differ slightly from the others, but all these characters, without exception, exemplify a discrepancy between what they esteem themselves to be and what they really are—by nature, by the circumstances others force on them, or by a combination of the two. . . .

Julius Caesar thus dramatizes human failure by stressing the unsatisfactory reality man experiences despite his grandiose dreams. . . . What the characters of *Julius Caesar* exemplify can be described as a contrast between what they esteem themselves to be and what they really are, between their false and their true selves, between dream and reality. The action of the play, however, is such that the condition its characters exemplify is more accurately described as a contrast involving not only the opposition between what they esteem themselves to be and what they really are but also the additional and more prominent opposition between their aspirations and what really happens to them. The 'unsatisfactory reality' man experiences despite his grandiose dreams has also another and perhaps better name: it is 'history.'

Julius Caesar, with its notorious clock, may not always *be* good history, but it is very much about history, and almost explicitly so. Cassius' anticipation of future plays on the assassination, for example, is a challenge to the spectators to compare his assumptions with the facts and attitudes they have acquired through their familiarity with history, and most of them will necessarily realize that while Cassius represents things one way, history has represented them in quite another. More important, however, is the fact that Cassius' challenge prompts the spectators to become aware of the phenomenon of history in itself, so that it becomes a valid, almost conscious element of their experience of the play. Much the same thing occurs on each of the numerous occasions when a character prophesies about the future, which for the audience is the past, something that history has already settled, usually in such a way that the character is proven wrong. And, given this context, much the same thing probably occurs every time one of the characters whose historical career is especially familiar conveys any assumption about himself that does not coincide with the way things have actually turned out, any time he plays the role conceived by his own self-esteem rather than the role written for him by history.

OCTAVIUS THE ONLY ONE WHO DOES NOT ROLE PLAY

Cassius, who began with the belief that man has full control over his destiny, eventually comes to realize that 'the affairs

of men rest still incertain' (v.i.95). A few minutes later, as the
battle of Philippi is about to begin; Brutus expresses his
anxiety about the outcome:

> O that a man might know
> The end of this day's business ere it come!
> But it sufficeth that the day will end,
> And then the end is known.

(122–5)

Cassius' change of mind and Brutus' suggestion that the outcome of an event is somehow autonomous record their partial realizations that history is an active force operating in-
dependently of the wills of individual men. Shakespeare
dramatizes this idea of history by constantly keeping his
spectators aware of history as a phenomenon while they
watch his play. He also manages to embody the force of history in one of the concrete elements of the action. The last
character to gain prominence in *Julius Caesar* is the only important character not participating in the discrepant role-
playing. Octavius Caesar remains exempt from the ironic
contrast between dream and reality because he has no imag-
ined conception of himself which the reality of history can
mock. He does not, like Caesar or Brutus, assume a manner
foreign to his true nature, nor does he, like Cassius, betray
aspirations not in harmony with his accomplishments. . . .
Octavius Caesar simply acts: he exists only in and as his accomplishment, which is the accomplishment of the historical Octavius Caesar. He is therefore less a character than an
embodiment of history. As an agent in the narrative design,
he prevents Antony from fulfilling his aspirations; as an element of the symbolic design he represents the force that
trips up all the others. . . .

The last speech, properly enough, goes to Octavius Caesar. *Julius Caesar,* as a result, though categorized as a tragedy, proves to be more truly a history play than those ordi-
narily so designated. They are history plays chiefly in the
sense that they take their subjects from English history, but
they would more accurately be described as plays about
kingship. *Julius Caesar,* on the other hand, takes history itself as subject by dramatizing it as an active force. Unlike
most history plays, by Shakespeare or others, *Julius Caesar*
is actually a play *about* history.

Manifestations of the Supernatural in *Julius Caesar*

Cumberland Clark

The Romans were extremely superstitious people who put great store in prodigies (i.e., omens, portents, supernatural signs), ghosts, dreams, astrology, and other fantastic elements. Shakespeare faithfully worked a number of these elements into his most famous Roman play, *Julius Caesar*. The late Cumberland Clark, former vice-president of the Shakespeare Reading Society and a prolific author on Shakespeare's works, here presents a spirited look at the ways the playwright used the theme of the supernatural in telling the tale of mighty Caesar's fall. After providing an excellent description of the setting and appearance of Caesar's ghost, Clark makes the point that in life Caesar was not nearly as formidable as he was in death. Then Clark discusses omens, including the storm in which Casca and Cicero meet, as well as the serious and often fearful manner in which the characters react to disturbing dreams.

While a study of Shakespeare and the Supernatural necessarily concerns itself chiefly with the four great dramas in which fairies, ghosts, and witches play a principal part, there are at least a dozen others from which the poet was unable to exclude the influences of the unseen world. Probably the most famous of these is *Julius Caesar*.

A tragedy dealing with the conflict between monarchical and democratic parties in the political world of Rome may seem a somewhat unpromising stage on which to introduce the Supernatural. It must be remembered, however, that the Romans were extremely superstitious, a trait that is emphasized over and over again in *Julius Caesar*. The marvellous and unnatural are

Reprinted from *Shakespeare and the Supernatural*, by Cumberland Clark (London: Williams & Norgate, 1931).

not represented solely by the appearance of Caesar's Ghost in IV. 3. They are given special prominence by the terrifying astrological portents that accompany the storm on the eve of the assassination, the prophetic dream of Calphurnia, and the warnings uttered by Artemidorus and the Soothsayer.

AN UNUSUAL AND EERIE EXPERIENCE

Perhaps Shakespeare would not have introduced the principal supernatural event–the appearance of the Ghost–if he had not found it in his authority, Plutarch. The Greek biographer describes in uninspired language the circumstances and manner of the spectral visit, and goes on to say, "Brutus boldly asked what he was, a god or a man, and what cause brought him hither? The spirit answered: 'I am thy evil spirit, Brutus, and thou shalt see me by the city of Philippi.' Brutus being not otherwise afraid, replied again unto it: 'Well: then I shall see thee again.' The spirit presently vanished away."

This somewhat matter-of-fact account of an unusual phenomenon was transformed–as was all of Plutarch–into something impressive and dramatic by the master touch of Shakespeare. The Poet realized that the circumstances were favourable for some unusual and eerie experience. It was late at night and dark. Great events were pending. The memory of a crime, as yet unpunished and unavenged, hovered about the tent of Brutus. The republican leader has had a tiring day. He has just emerged from a violent quarrel with his brother-in-law, Cassius. He has received news of the death of his beloved and noble wife, Portia. His cause is not going well. Octavius and Antony are marching against him with a powerful army. He is tired and drowsy and troubled by a premonition of his own death at Philippi. His page, Lucius, has dozed off in the middle of playing to him "a sleepy tune." He tries to settle himself to read, when the Ghost, for whose appearance the music has helped to prepare the audience, enters (IV. 3. 275-281):

> *Bru.* How ill this taper burns! Ha! Who comes here?
> I think it is the weakness of mine eyes
> That shapes this monstrous apparition.
> It comes upon me.
> Art thou any thing?
> Art thou some god, some angel, or some devil,
> That makest my blood cold, and my hair to stare?
> Speak to me what thou art.

Thereafter Shakespeare transcribes Plutarch to the exit of the spectre.

Caesar's Ghost is a conventional ghost judged by Elizabethan superstition. It arrives in the depth of the night, heralded by solemn music, and must be addressed before it can speak. Like other ghosts, it is condemned to walk the earth until its death is avenged. Shakespeare's mind was very much upon these disturbing visitors at this period, for *Julius Caesar* and *Hamlet* were written much about the same time.

THE POWER AND INFLUENCE OF CAESAR'S SPIRIT

There is, however, a difference between Caesar's Ghost and the *Hamlet* Ghost. Caesar's Ghost is subjective. It appears only to Brutus. Hamlet's Ghost, on the other hand, is objective—it only becomes subjective on its later visit—and is seen by all present. Caesar's Ghost is more like the ghost of Banquo [in *Macbeth*]. Both Macbeth and Brutus recognize the subjective nature of the apparition before their eyes. Macbeth knows it is an "unreal mockery," the very painting of his fear; and Brutus declares "it is the weakness of mine eyes" that "shapes this monstrous apparition."

In the two plays, *Macbeth* and *Julius Caesar*, Shakespeare deals with the assassination of the head of state, and is not so interested in the one slain as in the results of the crime upon the murderer. In picturing these results he has found the Supernatural (suggested in each case by his authority) of the highest dramatic value. Julius Caesar alive is not a character that commands great respect and admiration. He is vain, boastful, irresolute, and a prey to flatterers. But Julius Caesar dead is an all-important influence in the drama. We are conscious throughout of the ever-presence of his restless, inexorable spirit hovering, like the Weird Sisters of *Macbeth*, over the whole action, and leading the assassins relentlessly to final doom and retribution. Brutus feels the power of the dead Caesar constantly. Even he, the hero of the tragedy, cannot escape from it. He cries (v. 3. 94–96):

O Julius Caesar, thou art mighty yet!
Thy spirit walks abroad, and turns our swords
In our own proper entrails.

Marc Antony expresses the same thought (III. 3. 270–275):

. . . Caesar's spirit ranging for revenge,
With Ate by his side, come hot from hell,
Shall in these confines with a monarch's voice

> Cry "Havoc," and let slip the dogs of war;
> That this foul deed shall smell above the earth
> With carrion men, groaning for burial.

There is no doubt, I think, that Shakespeare meant us to understand that when the inward voice warns Brutus that his end is near, then his consciousness of the ever-presence of Caesar's spirit is so intensified that it brings him into closer contact with the Unseen and results in a visible manifestation.

When Caesar's Ghost tells Brutus that he will see him at Philippi (IV. 3. 283), he means that he will meet him on the same plane of existence—in other words, in the spirit world of the hereafter. Shakespeare, with his customary economy in the use of the Supernatural, does not show us this further spectral appearance on the stage; but we learn that it has happened from Brutus' speech to Volumnius (v. 5. 17–20):

> The ghost of Caesar hath appear'd to me
> Two several times by night; at Sardis once,
> And this last night here in Philippi fields:
> I know my hour is come.

Brutus seems to interpret the second manifestation as a command from the spirit of his victim to take his own life. Wherefore he runs upon his sword, and dies, exclaiming, "Caesar, now be still" (v. 5. 50).

PORTENTS AND DREAMS

Superstitious fear is wonderfully depicted by Shakespeare in the horror of Casca at the terrifying violence of the thunderstorm in I. 3, and the ghastly prodigies accompanying it—all intended as a sign of the anger of the gods at the dastardly conspiracy against Caesar. To an Elizabethan audience, steeped as it was in astrology, these celestial disturbances would bear a profound significance. Only the level-headedness of Cicero prevents Casca from becoming panic-stricken, until the shrewd Cassius arrives to place an interpretation upon the phenomena that appears to justify the dark conspiracy against Caesar. Here we have an instance of the *friendly* intervention of the Supernatural in an endeavour to prevent man from committing blunders that will prove disastrous to himself. Man, however, cannot be deprived of his freewill and independence, even when such deprivation would be to his own advantage. He can choose to ignore the helpful warning from the metaphysical world, silencing it with his own obstinacy and wilfulness. This course the conspirators against Caesar pursue, and eventually pay for their mistake with their lives.

Much store was laid by Shakespeare's contemporaries on dreams and their interpretation. Here was a favourite channel of communication between the mortal and immortal, and free use was made of it by the playwrights. Calphurnia's dream (II 2) would strike the average playgoer as a clear warning from the spirit world which no sensible man should ignore.

We learn of Calphurnia's troubled sleep in the first lines of the scene. Caesar says:

> Nor heaven nor earth have been at peace to-night
> Thrice hath Calphurnia in her sleep cried out,
> "Help, ho ! They murder Caesar!"

But the first arguments that Caesar's wife uses to dissuade her husband from leaving their house on the fatal day are the violent thunderstorm and the "horrid sights" which accompanied it. . . . To these Caesar turns a deaf ear. He is terribly afraid of being thought afraid. But Calphurnia's pleading is insistent. She tells him, "Your wisdom is consumed in confidence", and on bended knee begs him to call it *her* fear, and not his own, that keeps him at home. Caesar is persuaded; but at that moment, unfortunately, the wily conspirator, Decius, arrives to learn of his decision. Realizing at once that it must involve the utter failure of the conspiracy, he presses Caesar to give him the reason for absenting himself from the senate-house. It is then we hear of Calphurnia's dream in detail. . . . With remarkable presence of mind and ingenuity Decius places an entirely new and favourable construction on the dream, and one that flatters Caesar. He tells the dictator that the Senate intend to offer him a royal crown, and is scornful that this final triumph of his career should be frustrated by the foolish fears of a weak woman. Caesar is persuaded to change his mind once again. . . . He waves aside her presentiment and allows his vanity to lead him to his death. Caesar's action in rejecting so clear an offer of metaphysical aid would sound like madness in Elizabethan ears, and would fill the audience with excited anticipation of the inevitable penalty.

WARNINGS THAT GO UNHEEDED

Another hand from the Unseen is outstretched to save Caesar. Through Artemidorus and a Soothsayer further warnings are given of the danger threatening him. Prophecy was one of the recognized branches of witchcraft; and the picture of Caesar recklessly turning from these well-intentioned and clairvoyant counsellors would be, in the modern phrase, "good theatre."

Although the Supernatural is not dominant in *Julius Caesar*, it has an important role to fill in the unfoldment of the tragedy. It intervenes in an endeavour to prevent men from committing irrevocable blunders. But it fails, for it has no power to coerce the free-will of man. Its warnings are disregarded, and disaster ensues.

Shakespeare's Use of Blood Imagery in the Play

Maurice Charney

Even the most casual examination of *Julius Caesar*
reveals that the play abounds with verbal references
to blood, as well as often vivid visual allusions to
blood and blood-letting. In this excerpt from his pen-
etrating study of the play's imagery, noted Shakespearean expert, Maurice Charney, explores many
of these allusions. He concludes, for instance, that
blood is the chief symbol of the conspiracy. Moreover, says Charney, the conspirators view the blood-
letting of the assassination as a kind of ritual purification in which the evils infecting Rome (represented by Caesar's dictatorship) are purged. As the
play's later events demonstrate, of course, this view
turns out to be mostly self-deceptive. Similarly, images of blood underscore Brutus's tragedy, his sincere belief that his betrayal of Caesar is a noble act,
when in reality it is a misguided one. In the end,
Charney suggests, the cry of the timeless, primitive
blood feud, "blood for blood," echoes once again, as
Brutus and the other conspirators pay for spilling
Caesar's blood by forfeiting their own.

The central issue about the meaning of *Julius Caesar* is
raised most forcefully and vividly by the imagery of blood. If
the murder of Caesar is indeed a "savage spectacle"
(3.1.223), then the blood with which the conspirators are
smeared "Up to the elbows" (3.1.107) is the sign of their
guilt. But if the murder of Caesar is a ritual blood-letting of
the body politic of Rome, then blood is the sign of purification and new life. The latter point of view marks the tragedy
of Brutus, for he cannot foresee that his high-minded but

Reprinted by permission of the publisher from *Shakespeare's Roman Plays*, by Maurice
Charney (Cambridge, MA: Harvard University Press). Copyright © 1961 by the Presi-
dent and Fellows of Harvard College.

specious motives will be drowned in the bloodiness of murder and civil strife. He is tragically unable to bridge the gap between reasons and acts.

THE STAIN OF BRUTUS'S GUILT

The blood theme begins in II,i, where it becomes a powerful symbol for the conspiracy. The question of what to do with Antony after the murder of Caesar is a crucial one. The shrewd and practical Cassius wants to kill him, but Brutus objects and makes, according to Plutarch, the first great tactical error of his career. This decision also indicates the rift between the other conspirators and Brutus, who argues his position from the analogy between the bodies human and politic:

> Our course will seem too bloody, Caius Cassius,
> To cut the head off and then hack the limbs,
> Like wrath in death and envy afterwards;
> For Antony is but a limb of Caesar.

(2.1.162–65)

He thinks of blood as the symbol of common murder, and he fears the stain of its guilt. The slaying of Caesar is a necessary and beneficial act, but Brutus wishes that there were no blood:

> Let's be sacrificers, but not butchers, Caius.
> We all stand up against the spirit of Caesar,
> And in the spirit of men there is no blood.
> O that we then could come by Caesar's spirit
> And not dismember Caesar! But, alas,
> Caesar must bleed for it!

(2.1.166–71)

This is one of the most important passages in the play for showing the tragic wrongness of Brutus. The murder of Caesar proves to be not a loving sacrifice, but only a fruitless act of butchery. . . . When all is done, only the body of Caesar has been killed, not the spirit, which stays very much alive in Antony and Octavius and wins vengeance in civil strife. The meaning of the play can almost be formulated by taking the negative of all these statements of Brutus.

The tragedy of Brutus springs from his complete sincerity in preferring duty to Rome to his personal friendship with Caesar. In this sense his tragic course is ironic because his choice is essentially noble but misguided. It is an irony of his situation that things turn out quite differently from what he had anticipated. His inner conflicts are still strong in these early scenes, and it is from his paradoxically divided loyalties that he speaks of the murder of Caesar as a loving, sacrificial act:

> And, gentle friends,
> Let's kill him boldly, but not wrathfully;
> Let's carve him as a dish fit for the gods,
> Not hew him as a carcass fit for hounds.
> And let our hearts, as subtle masters do,
> Stir up their servants to an act of rage
> And after seem to chide 'em. This shall make
> Our purpose necessary, and not envious;
> Which so appearing to the common eyes,
> We shall be call'd purgers, not murderers.
>
> (2.1.171–80)

Brutus persists in the analogy of the state as a body, which the conspirators by bleeding will restore to health. In this way the assassination of Caesar will be a purgation, a phlebotomy, and not a murder—it is a necessary though bloody act, and Brutus shrinks from the bloody stain of murder.

THE BLOOD FLOWS FREELY

Among the portents in the next scene are two powerful signs of blood. Calphurnia warns Caesar of "Fierce fiery warriors" (2.2.19) who "drizzled blood upon the Capitol" (2.2.21). This blood prepares us for the actual murder of Caesar in the Capitol, and "Fierce fiery warriors" looks ahead to the antagonists in the civil strife. The concern with blood becomes more ominous in Calphurnia's dream, as Caesar relates it to Decius:

> She dreamt to-night she saw my statuë,
> Which, like a fountain with an hundred spouts,
> Did run pure blood; and many lusty Romans
> Came smiling and did bathe their hands in it.
>
> (2.2.76–79)

This image, too, anticipates the later action in which the conspirators do actually bathe their hands in Caesar's blood after his murder. But Decius turns Calphurnia's dream to seemingly favorable omen:

> Your statue spouting blood in many pipes,
> In which so many smiling Romans bath'd,
> Signifies that from you great Rome shall suck
> Reviving blood, and that great men shall press
> For tinctures, stains, relics, and cognizance.
>
> (2.2.85–89)

The image continues the analogy between Caesar's body and the body politic of Rome. There is a covert praise of Cae-

sar's assassination here: the body politic of Rome will be re-
vived by the murder of Caesar, although great men will
press for memorials of him once he is dead. The last two
lines are full of heraldic and religious imagery intended to
flatter Caesar.

Blood imagery is of greatest importance in III,i, where it is
not only a repeated verbal theme, but also enters into the stage
action. Animal blood from concealed bladders or sponges was
probably used to represent Caesar's murder on the Elizabethan
stage, and, from all indications, there was a frank emphasis on
the spectacular effects of murder scenes. . . .

A number of blood images in III,i show Caesar in the height
of pride just before his fall. He thrusts aside Metellus Cimber,
who "might fire the blood of ordinary men" (3.1.37), but not
Caesar's. He does not bear "such rebel blood" (3.1.40) that can
be melted by emotional persuasion, and the chief connotation of
"blood" is the passion that Caesar forswears. The world is full of
men who are "flesh and blood, and apprehensive" (3.1.67), but
only Caesar remains in cold, unchanging constancy. Yet ten
lines later he is stabbed to death as readily as any mortal, and
the blood that would not be fired or thawed now flows freely
from the dagger wounds of the conspirators.

A Fearful Blood Ritual

From this point until the end of the play the fact of Caesar's assassination is kept constantly before the audience, and this is
done to a large extent by blood imagery. Of course, Caesar's
bloody and rent body is on stage through all of this scene, and
at a number of important moments (3.1.148–50, 194–210,
254–75) Antony addresses it as if it were a living presence; Octavius' Servant does the same (3.1.281). In the next scene it is
absent only for the short time of Brutus' oration. At line 44
Antony and others enter with the body, which remains on
stage until removed by the plebeians for the funeral pyre.
Thus Caesar's body dominates the scene for almost 450 lines
after his death. The body plays a conspicuous role during
Antony's funeral oration, but throughout the time it is on stage
it serves as a visible indictment of the conspirators. Its com-
manding presence on stage, possibly on the elevated platform
or dais on which the "throne" usually stood, keeps the audience aware of the crime of assassination.

Shortly after the murder, Brutus directs the conspirators
in a fearful blood ritual:

Shakespeare's Use of Blood Imagery in the Play   159

> Stoop, Romans, stoop,
> And let us bathe our hands in Caesar's blood
> Up to the elbows and besmear our swords.
> Then walk we forth, even to the market place,
> And waving our red weapons o'er our heads,
> Let's all cry 'Peace, freedom, and liberty!'
>
> (3.1.105–10)

This action fulfills the prophecy of Calphurnia's dream (2.2.76–79), and we may assume that stage blood was liberally used for these effects, since the conspirators' hands and swords need to remain very vividly bloody for about 150 lines (until the exit at 3.1.253). The blood ritual that Brutus began at 2.I.166 seems now a sacrilege rather than a consecration. It is continued as Cassius takes up Brutus' invocation:

> Stoop then and wash. How many ages hence
> Shall this our lofty scene be acted over
> In states unborn and accents yet unknown!
>
> (3.1.111–13)

And Brutus answers . . . in the same spirit of uncontrolled exaltation:

> How many times shall Caesar bleed in sport,
> That now on Pompey's basis lies along
> No worthier than the dust!
>
> (3.1.114–16)

The eyes of the conspirators are on posterity, which they are sure will approve their present acts. These speeches represent the highest point in the development of the conspirators; with the entrance of Antony's Servant their downward course begins.

BODY, BLOOD, AND SPIRIT INSEPARABLE

Antony's speeches in this scene reiterate "blood" both as the symbol of the murdered Caesar and as the sign of the conspirators' guilt. The double emphasis is made almost in his first words:

> I know not, gentlemen, what you intend,
> Who else must be let blood, who else is rank.
> If I myself, there is no hour so fit
> As Caesar's death's hour; nor no instrument
> Of half that worth as those your swords, made rich
> With the most noble blood of all this world.
> I do beseech ye, if you bear me hard,
> Now, whilst your purpled hands do reek and smoke,
> Fulfil your pleasure.
>
> (3.1.151–59)

Antony's thoughts run on blood as he boldly dares the conspirators to kill him, too. Their hands and swords have been bathed in Caesar's blood, whose visual signs they now flaunt to all Rome as justification of their deed. Throughout this scene Antony provides a bitter, sarcastic commentary on these "purpled hands" and swords, for they bear the stain of guilt upon them. . . .

Brutus' reply to Antony acknowledges the blood, but attempts to offer reasons:

> O Antony, beg not your death of us!
> Though now we must appear bloody and cruel,
> As by our hands and this our present act
> You see we do, yet see you but our hands
> And this the bleeding business they have done.
> Our hearts you see not. They are pitiful. . . .
>
> (3.1.164–69)

The separation of "hands" from "hearts" echoes Brutus' earlier distinction between the body and the spirit of Caesar (2.1.166ff). In his tragic blindness he cannot see that the one ("hands") is not simply an instrument for the other ("hearts"): in the act of murder the body and its blood are inseparable from the spirit.

But it is the bloody hands of the conspirators that Antony is insisting on as the outward badge of their guilt. In a supremely ironic ceremony Antony shakes each of their hands:

> Let each man render me his bloody hand.
> First, Marcus Brutus, will I shake with you;
> Next, Caius Cassius, do I take your hand;
> Now, Decius Brutus, yours; now yours, Metellus;
> Yours, Cinna; and, my valiant Casca, yours.
> Though last, not least in love, yours, good Trebonius.
>
> (3.1.184–89)

This ceremony parallels the one by which Brutus entered the conspiracy: "Give me your hands all over, one by one" (2.1.112). We need to supply the all-important expression and attitude of Antony here, the mingling of intense loathing and feigned reconciliation. From this handshaking Antony acquires "bloody fingers". . . and he speaks as if to undo the guilty ritual in which he has participated:

> Pardon me, Julius! Here wast thou bay'd, brave hart;
> Here didst thou fall; and here thy hunters stand,
> Sign'd in thy spoil, and crimson'd in thy lethe.
> O world, thou wast the forest to this hart;
> And this indeed, O world, the heart of thee!
> How like a deer, stroken by many princes,
> Dost thou here lie!
>
> (3.1.204–10)

He has almost gone too far . . . but Brutus, who himself loved Caesar, will now shield Antony. The hunting imagery of this speech stresses butchery rather than the sacrifice Brutus hoped for. . . . By sharing in Caesar's blood he [Antony] has seemed to condone the murder, but behind this mask vengeance for Caesar is being prepared.

ANTONY PROMISES "BLOOD AND DESTRUCTION"

Brutus' unshaken sense of his own rightness allows him to commit his second great tactical error according to Plutarch: he gives Antony permission to speak a funeral oration for Caesar in the market place. We need to understand the tragic character of Brutus here. He has absolute confidence in his own rational power, for the conflict in him does not go beyond the alignment of motives leading to the decision to murder Caesar:

> Between the acting of a dreadful thing
> And the first motion, all the interim is
> Like a phantasma or a hideous dream.
>
> (2.1.63–65)

After the "acting" of the "dreadful thing," however (equivalent to the decision to murder Caesar, rather than the murder itself), the "phantasma" and "hideous dream" become things external rather than aspects of Brutus' mind. . . . The scope of Brutus' tragedy is limited by his own sense of rightness, for his decision to take part in the conspiracy seems to end his process of self-questioning. He is "arm'd so strong in honesty" (4.3.67) that he cannot feel the world aright or admit the possibility of error, although the quarrel scene perhaps contains a subdued sense of guilt and tragic disillusion. He will either give reasons to Antony for Caesar's murder, "Or else were this a savage spectacle" (3.1.223). But Brutus seems too sure of his reasons to allow for alternatives to his own course of action, and this is one of the chief sources of his tragic blindness.

Antony's soliloquy after the conspirators leave says directly and forcefully what has already been said ironically. The stage situation for this soliloquy is particularly impressive. Beginning with the meeting of the Senate and continuing with the murder of Caesar and its aftermath, the stage has always been crowded, especially with conspirators. Antony's aloneness, then, comes as a sudden contrast. It is a moment of unexpected quiet which indicates that the counteraction is already underway. Antony apologizes to the dead Caesar for his conciliatory role with "these butchers" (3.1.255), and he prophesies the vengeance of blood for blood that must follow:

> Woe to the hand that shed this costly blood!
> Over thy wounds now do I prophesy
> (Which, like dumb mouths, do ope their ruby lips
> To beg the voice and utterance of my tongue),
> A curse shall light upon the limbs of men;
> Domestic fury and fierce civil strife
> Shall cumber all the parts of Italy;
> Blood and destruction shall be so in use
> And dreadful objects so familiar
> That mothers shall but smile when they behold
> Their infants quartered with the hands of war,
> All pity chok'd with custom of fell deeds. . . .
>
> (3.1.258–69)

In III,i we learn that Antony will use his funeral oration to see "how the people take / The cruel issue of these bloody men. . . " (3.1.293–94), and the oration never allows us to forget the blood of Caesar. If Antony read Caesar's will, the commons would "go and kiss dead Caesar's wounds / And dip their napkins in his sacred blood. . ." (3.2.138–39). This blood has now become that of a martyr or a saint. Brutus' "most unkindest cut of all" (3.2.188) burst Caesar's heart, and

> Even at the base of Pompey's statue
> (Which all the while ran blood) great Caesar fell.
>
> (3.2.193–94)

We recall Caesar's triumphing "over Pompey's blood" (1.1.56) at the beginning of the play; now Pompey triumphs over Caesar's blood. Antony very artfully disclaims any power as an orator "To stir men's blood" (3.2.228). The "most bloody sight" (3.2.207) of Caesar's body and "sweet Caesar's wounds, poor poor dumb mouths" (3.2.230) speak for themselves and act as a powerful persuasion to vengeance.

"BLOOD FOR BLOOD" IN THE FINALE

There is a general slackening of the blood imagery in Acts IV and V. After Brutus' "bloody spur" (4.2.25) image for the civil war, the next significant use of "blood" is in the quarrel scene. Brutus counters Cassius' waspish indignation with the fact of Caesar's murder:

> Remember March; the ides of March remember.
> Did not great Julius bleed for justice sake?
> What villain touch'd his body that did stab
> And not for justice?
>
> (4.3.18–21)

If the purpose of the assassination were not justice, then Caesar's blood is the mark of butchery and murder. By the time of this scene the first flush of idealism has gone out of the conspiracy. It is seen here on the defensive, and Cassius' venality is a sign of disillusion. Only Brutus persists in his original uprightness, which is repeatedly expressed with all the insolent frankness of the morally sure. There is also a suggestion here that Brutus is beginning to be aware of the tragic betrayal of the original ideals of the conspiracy. This awareness creates a sense of doom and fatality in the scene, which is climaxed by the appearance of Caesar's Ghost.

The blood imagery of V,i sets the tone for the battle of Philippi in V,ii. A Messenger reports the enemy's "bloody sign of battle" (5.1.14) to Antony and Octavius. Further on, Octavius cuts off the ingenious conceits of the battle parley with the words of a practical man:

> Come, come, the cause! If arguing make us sweat,
> The proof of it will turn to redder drops.
> Look,
> I draw a sword against conspirators.
> When think you that the sword goes up again?
> Never, till Caesar's three-and-thirty wounds
> Be well aveng'd, or till another Caesar
> Have added slaughter to the sword of traitors. (5.1.48–55)

This is the case against Brutus, Cassius, and their party: they are "conspirators" and "traitors" who must answer for it in battle; the arbitration of the issue will be in blood, not words. The final blood image is used by Titinius for the dead Cassius:

> O setting sun,
> As in thy red rays thou dost sink to night,
> So in his red blood Cassius' day is set!
> The sun of Rome is set. (5.3.60–63)

So Cassius ends in his own "red blood," slain by the same hand and with the same sword that stabbed Caesar. This is the reciprocity of blood for blood.

CHRONOLOGY

1543

Polish astronomer Nicolaus Copernicus introduces the idea of a sun-centered, rather than an earth-centered, universe in his *On the Revolutions.*

1557

William Shakespeare's parents, John Shakespeare and Mary Arden, are married.

1558

Elizabeth I becomes queen of England, initiating the so-called Elizabethan Age.

1564

William Shakespeare is born in the village of Stratford in central England; his noted contemporary, writer Christopher Marlowe, is also born.

1576

London's first public theater, called The Theatre, opens.

1577

Raphael Holinshed's *Chronicles,* which will become the source for many of Shakespeare's plays, appears.

1577–1580

Englishman Sir Francis Drake sails around the world.

1579

Englishman Sir Thomas North translates Plutarch's *Parallel Lives* from a French version, producing the first English version, *Lives of the Noble Grecians and Romans;* in the following few years Shakespeare becomes familiar with the work.

1582

William Shakespeare marries Anne Hathaway.

CA. 1587
Shakespeare leaves Stratford and heads for London to pursue a career in the theater.

1588
England wins a major victory over Spain by defeating the mighty Spanish Armada.

CA. 1590–1593
Shakespeare writes *Richard III, The Comedy of Errors,* and *Henry VI, Parts 1, 2,* and *3.*

1594
Shakespeare joins the newly formed Lord Chamberlain's Company theatrical troupe.

CA. 1594–1599
Shakespeare writes *The Taming of the Shrew; The Two Gentlemen of Verona; The Merry Wives of Windsor; Twelfth Night; Richard II; Henry IV, Parts 1* and *2;* and *Henry V.*

1599
Shakespeare writes *Julius Caesar,* basing much of the historical information on North's translation of Plutarch's history of the lives of Caesar, Brutus, and Antony; the play is first performed in the same year, probably in the fall.

CA. 1601–1607
Shakespeare writes what will later be acknowledged as his greatest tragedies, *Hamlet, Othello, King Lear, Macbeth,* and *Antony and Cleopatra.*

1603
Queen Elizabeth dies; James I becomes king of England; the English conquer Ireland.

1607
English settlers establish the colony of Jamestown in North America.

1611
The King James version of the Bible is published.

1616
Shakespeare dies.

1623
Anne Hathaway Shakespeare dies; the First Folio, a collection of Shakespeare's complete works, including *Julius Caesar* in its first printed version, is published.

CA. 1680–1710

Veteran Shakespearean actor Thomas Betterton plays Brutus in several well-received productions of *Julius Caesar.*

1683–1686

English literary great John Dryden publishes his translation of Plutarch's *Parallel Lives,* which eventually supercedes the North version in popularity and influence.

1794

The highly respected American actor Lewis Hallam plays Brutus.

1838

Acclaimed English actor-manager William Charles Macready stages a spectacular version of *Julius Caesar* at London's Covent Garden.

1871

American actor Edwin Booth, brother of John Wilkes Booth, assassin of Abraham Lincoln, plays Brutus in a large-scale New York production of *Julius Caesar.*

1937

Controversial American radio and stage actor-director Orson Welles presents his famous and subsequently highly influential "fascist" version of the play, a production staged in modern dress and subtitled "Death of a Dictator."

1953

MGM releases a well-reviewed film version of *Julius Caesar* directed by Joseph L. Mankiewicz and starring James Mason as Brutus, John Gielgud as Cassius, Marlon Brando as Antony, and Louis Calhern as Caesar.

1970

Another film version of *Julius Caesar* appears, this one directed by Stuart Burge and starring Charlton Heston as Antony, John Gielgud as Caesar, and Jason Robards as Brutus.

FOR FURTHER RESEARCH

JULIUS CAESAR'S LIFE, TIMES, AND HISTORICAL IMPORTANCE

Appian, *Roman History*. Trans. Horace White. Cambridge, MA: Harvard University Press, 1964.

Ernle Bradford, *Julius Caesar: The Pursuit of Power*. New York: Morrow, 1984.

Julius Caesar, *Commentaries on the Gallic War* and *Civil Wars*, published as *War Commentaries of Caesar*. Trans. Rex Warner. New York: New American Library, 1960.

Michael Crawford, *The Roman Republic*. Cambridge, MA: Harvard University Press, 1993.

Michael Grant, *Caesar*. London: Weidenfeld and Nicolson, 1974.

Christian Meier, *Caesar*. Trans. David McClintock. New York: HarperCollins, 1996.

Plutarch, *Parallel Lives*. Published complete: John Dryden trans., *Lives of the Noble Grecians and Romans*. New York: Random House, 1932. Excerpts published as: Rex Warner trans., *The Fall of the Roman Republic: Six Lives by Plutarch*. New York: Penguin Books, 1972; and Ian Scott-Kilvert trans., *Makers of Rome: Nine Lives by Plutarch*. New York: Penguin Books, 1965.

Suetonius, *Lives of the Twelve Caesars*, published as *The Twelve Caesars*. Trans. Robert Graves, rev. Michael Grant. New York: Penguin Books, 1979.

TEXT, ANALYSIS, AND CRITICISM OF SHAKESPEARE'S *JULIUS CAESAR*

John F. Andrews, ed., *Julius Caesar*. London: J.M. Dent, 1993.

David Bevington, ed., *Julius Caesar*. New York: Bantam Books, 1988.

E. Charlton Black, ed., *Julius Caesar*. Boston: Ginn, 1908.

Jan H. Blits, *The End of the Ancient Republic: Essays on* Julius Caesar. Durham, NC: Carolina Academic Press, 1982.

Adrien Bonjour, *The Structure of* Julius Caesar. Liverpool: Liverpool University Press, 1958.

Paul Cantor, *Shakespeare's Rome: Republic and Empire.* Ithaca, NY: Cornell University Press, 1976.

Maurice Charney, *Shakespeare's Roman Plays: The Function of Imagery in the Drama.* Cambridge, MA: Harvard University Press, 1961.

M.L. Clarke, *The Noblest Roman: Marcus Brutus and His Reputation.* Ithaca, NY: Cornell University Press, 1981.

Leonard F. Dean, ed., *Twentieth Century Interpretations of* Julius Caesar. Englewood Cliffs, NJ: Prentice-Hall, 1968.

Albert Furtwangler, *Assassin on Stage: Brutus, Hamlet, and the Death of Lincoln.* Chicago: University of Illinois Press, 1991.

Harley Granville-Barker, *Prefaces to Shakespeare, Vol. 2:* King Lear, Cymbeline, Julius Caesar. Princeton, NJ: Princeton University Press, 1963.

G.B. Harrison, *Julius Caesar in Shakespeare, Shaw, and the Ancients.* New York: Harcourt, Brace, and World, 1960.

Arthur Humphreys, ed., *Julius Caesar.* Oxford, England: Clarendon Press, 1984.

Alexander Leggatt, *Shakespeare's Political Drama: The History Plays and the Roman Plays.* London: Methuen, 1988.

Robert S. Miola, *Shakespeare's Rome.* Cambridge: Cambridge University Press, 1983.

John Ripley, Julius Caesar *on Stage in England and America, 1599–1973.* Cambridge: Cambridge University Press, 1980.

Norman Sanders, ed., *Julius Caesar.* New York: Penguin Books, 1967.

Paul N. Siegel, *Shakespeare's English and Roman History Plays.* Rutherford, NJ: Fairleigh Dickinson University Press, 1986.

F.L. Simmons, *Shakespeare's Pagan World: The Roman Tragedies.* Charlottesville: University Press of Virginia, 1973.

T.J.B. Spencer, *Shakespeare's Plutarch.* New York: Penguin Books, 1964.

Derek Traversi, *Shakespeare: The Roman Plays.* Stanford, CA: Stanford University Press, 1963.

Richard Wilson, *Julius Caesar.* New York: Penguin Books, 1992.

Louis B. Wright and Virginia A. LaMar, eds., *Julius Caesar.* 1959. Reprint, New York: Simon and Schuster, 1970.

SHAKESPEARE'S LIFE AND TIMES

Marchette Chute, *Shakespeare of London.* New York: E.P. Dutton, 1949.

Roland M. Frye, *Shakespeare's Life and Times: A Pictorial Record.* Princeton, NJ: Princeton University Press, 1967.

François Laroque, *The Age of Shakespeare.* New York: Harry N. Abrams, 1993.

Peter Levi, *The Life and Times of William Shakespeare.* New York: Henry Holt, 1989.

A.A. Mendilow and Alice Shalvi, *The World and Art of Shakespeare.* New York: Daniel Davey, 1967.

Peter Quennell, *Shakespeare: A Biography.* Cleveland: World, 1963.

A.L. Rowse, *Shakespeare the Man.* New York: Harper and Row, 1973.

SHAKESPEAREAN THEATER, FILM, AND ACTORS

John C. Adams, *The Globe Playhouse: Its Design and Equipment.* Cambridge, MA: Harvard University Press, 1942.

Ivor Brown, *Shakespeare and the Actors.* New York: Coward-McCann, 1970.

Charles W. Eckert, *Focus on Shakespearean Films.* Englewood Cliffs, NJ: Prentice-Hall, 1972.

Richard France, ed., *Orson Welles on Shakespeare: The W.P.A. and Mercury Theater Playscripts.* Westport, CT: Greenwood Press, 1990.

John Gielgud, *An Actor and His Times.* London: Sidgwick and Jackson, 1979.

G.B. Harrison, *Elizabethan Plays and Players.* Ann Arbor: University of Michigan Press, 1956.

Charlton Heston, *Into the Arena: An Autobiography.* New York: Simon and Schuster, 1995.

Roger Manvell, *Shakespeare and the Film.* London: Debt, 1971.

Laurence Olivier, *On Acting.* Weidenfeld and Nicolson, 1986.

GENERAL GUIDES TO SHAKESPEARE'S PLAYS

Charles Boyce, *Shakespeare: A to Z: The Essential Reference to His Plays, His Poems, His Life and Times, and More.* New York: Facts On File, 1990.

Marchette Chute, *Stories from Shakespeare.* New York: New American Library, 1956.

Norrie Epstein, *The Friendly Shakespeare: A Thoroughly Painless Guide to the Best of the Bard.* New York: Viking Penguin, 1993.

Harley Granville-Barker and G.B. Harrison, eds., *A Companion to Shakespeare Studies.* Cambridge: Cambridge University Press, 1959.

Karl J. Holzknecht, *The Backgrounds of Shakespeare's Plays.* New York: American Books, 1950.

Kenneth Muir, *The Sources of Shakespeare's Plays.* New Haven, CT: Yale University Press, 1978.

Kenneth Muir and Samuel Schoenbaum, eds., *A New Companion to Shakespeare Studies.* Oxford: Oxford University Press, 1971.

The Riverside Shakespeare. Boston: Houghton Mifflin, 1974.

GENERAL SHAKESPEAREAN ANALYSIS AND CRITICISM

Andrew C. Bradley, *Shakespearean Tragedy.* New York: Viking Penguin, 1991.

Lily B. Campbell, *Shakespeare's Tragic Heroes: Slaves of Passion.* 1930. Reprint, New York: Barnes and Noble, 1968.

Edmund K. Chambers, *William Shakespeare: A Study of Facts and Problems.* New York: Oxford University Press, 1989.

Cumberland Clark, *Shakespeare and the Supernatural.* London: Williams and Norgate, 1931.

William Empson, *Essays on Shakespeare.* New York: Cambridge University Press, 1986.

M.D. Faber, *The Design Within: Psychoanalytic Approaches to Shakespeare.* New York: Science House, 1970.

Brian Gibbons, *Shakespeare and Multiplicity.* Cambridge: Cambridge University Press, 1993.

Philip H. Highfill, ed., *Shakespeare's Craft, Eight Lectures.* Carbondale: Southern Illinois University Press, 1982.

E.A.J. Honigmann, *Myriad-Minded Shakespeare: Essays on the Tragedies, Problem Comedies, and Shakespeare the Man.* New York: St. Martin's Press, 1998.

Carolyn R.S. Lenz et al., eds., *The Woman's Part: Feminist Criticism of Shakespeare.* Urbana: University of Illinois Press, 1980.

Dieter Mehl, *Shakespeare's Tragedies: An Introduction.* New York: Cambridge University Press, 1986.

Hugh M. Richmond, *Shakespeare's Political Plays.* New York: Random House, 1967.

Clarice Swisher, ed., *Readings on the Tragedies of William Shakespeare.* San Diego: Greenhaven Press, 1996.

James A.K. Thomson, *Shakespeare and the Classics.* Westport, CT: Greenwood Press, 1978.

Thomas F. Van Laan, *Role-Playing in Shakespeare.* Toronto: University of Toronto Press, 1978.

WORKS BY WILLIAM SHAKESPEARE

Editor's Note: Many of the dates on this list are approximate. Because manuscripts identified with the date of writing do not exist, scholars have determined the most accurate available date, either of the writing or of the first production of each play.

1 Henry VI (1591)

2 and *3 Henry VI* (1591–1592)

The Comedy of Errors; Richard III; Sonnets (1592–1593)

Titus Andronicus; The Taming of the Shrew; The Two Gentlemen of Verona; Love's Labour's Lost; publication of *Venus and Adonis* (1593)

Publication of *The Rape of Lucrece* (1594)

A Midsummer Night's Dream; Romeo and Juliet; Richard II (1594–1595)

The Merchant of Venice (1595–1596)

King John (1596)

1 Henry IV (1597)

2 Henry IV; Much Ado About Nothing (1598)

Henry V; As You Like It; Julius Caesar; The Merry Wives of Windsor; publication of "The Passionate Pilgrim" (1599)

Twelfth Night; Hamlet; Troilus and Cressida (1600–1601)

"The Phoenix and the Turtle" (1601)

Othello (1602)

All's Well That Ends Well (1603)

Measure for Measure (1604)

King Lear; Macbeth (1606)

Antony and Cleopatra; Coriolanus; Timon of Athens (unfinished); *Pericles* (1607–1609)

Sonnets and "A Lover's Complaint" first published by Thomas Thorpe (1609)

Cymbeline (1610)

The Winter's Tale (1610–1611)

The Tempest (1611)

Henry VIII (1612–1613)

Index

172